The Myth of Economic Development

T0056561

Critical South

The publication of this series is supported by the International Consortium of Critical Theory Programs funded by the Andrew W. Mellon Foundation.

Series editors: Natalia Brizuela and Leticia Sabsay

The Myth of Economic Development

Celso Furtado

Translated by Jordan B. Jones

polity

Originally published in Portuguese as *O mito do desenvolvimento econômico*
© André Tosi Furtado and Mario Tosi Furtado

This English edition © 2020 by Polity Press

Polity Press
65 Bridge Street
Cambridge CB2 1UR, UK

Polity Press
101 Station Landing
Suite 300
Medford, MA 02155, USA

ISBN-13: 978-1-5095-4013-6
ISBN-13: 978-1-5095-4014-3 (paperback)

Cover image:
Sandra Cinto
Untitled (from the series By Chance and Necessity) (detail)
2015
Permanent pen and acrylic on canvas
78 3/4 x 59 inches; 198.1 x 149.9 cm
Courtesy the artist and Tanya Bonakdar Gallery, New York / Los Angeles

A catalogue record for this book is available from the British Library.

Typeset in 10.5 on 12.5pt Sabon
by Fakenham Prepress Solutions, Fakenham, Norfolk NR21 8NL
Printed and bound in Great Britain by TJ International Limited

The publisher has used its best endeavours to ensure that the URLs for external websites referred to in this book are correct and active at the time of going to press. However, the publisher has no responsibility for the websites and can make no guarantee that a site will remain live or that the content is or will remain appropriate.

Every effort has been made to trace all copyright holders, but if any have been overlooked the publisher will be pleased to include any necessary credits in any subsequent reprint or edition.

For further information on Polity, visit our website:
politybooks.com

Contents

Introduction

Celso Furtado is one of the most influential intellectuals of his generation. Born in 1920 in northeastern Brazil, he had a prolific academic career punctuated by professional experiences in Brazil's central government.

Early on, during secondary school years, he was influenced by Positivism, especially the idea that science is the ultimate form of knowledge and that it can contribute to progress. The Marxist conception that social forms are human creations that can be transcended also left a strong impression on him. It made him understand that things are not immutable and that he could hope one day to see improvements in the socioeconomic situation of the northeastern part of his country. As a rather socially privileged teenager, he grew up in an environment of endemic poverty where the violence and the tyranny of men competed with the whims of nature (Furtado 1973).

In 1944, he graduated from the Federal University of Rio de Janeiro where he studied law, somewhat out of his family tradition, before reorienting himself toward administration, in order to strengthen his knowledge of organizational issues. Such an interest stemmed from the cardinal importance he attached to planning. This led him to pursue studies in economics in France, which culminated in a doctorate in 1948. His thesis focused on the history of the Brazilian colonial economy.

Between 1949 and 1957, he worked as an economist at the Economic Commission for Latin America (ECLA) in Chile. This allowed him to become immersed in the economic challenges of Latin America. There he became familiar with the ideas of Raúl Prebisch, who appointed him Head of the Economic Development Division. In particular, he took over the concepts of "center" and "periphery" from him. The "center" refers to the economies that form the heart of the capitalist system—the industrialized/developed countries—while the periphery is made up of the rest, the underdeveloped countries—those that specialize in exporting primary products and importing manufactured goods. As the first director of UNCTAD (United Nations Conference on Trade and Development) from its inception in 1964, Prebisch became famous for his thesis of a secular decline in the terms of trade between the countries of the center and those of the periphery. Numerous other intellectual influences fed Furtado's thinking, including the "decisive" influence of John Maynard Keynes, who enabled him to understand that the functioning of capitalism requires a significant degree of centralization of economic decisions (Furtado 1973; Kay 2005; Seccareccia & Correa 2014).

Between 1957 and 1958, at the invitation of the economist Nicholas Kaldor, whom he had met two years earlier, he spent an academic stay in Cambridge, UK, where he wrote *The Economic Growth of Brazil*, which became a classic. Then he was back home to be appointed

Director of the Brazilian Bank of Economic Development before taking charge of SUDENE (Superintendency for the Development of the Northeast): the federal agency in charge of the development of northeastern Brazil. He later became Brazil's first Minister of Planning (1962–1963). From 1964 on, the dictatorship deprived him of his political rights and forced him into exile for a decade. He was Professor of Development Economics at the Sorbonne (Paris) between 1965 and 1985. During these two decades, he had the opportunity to complete several academic stays abroad: he was a research fellow at Yale University (1964–1965), visiting professor at the American University (1972), visiting professor at Cambridge University (1973–1974), visiting professor at the Catholic University of Sao Paulo, Brazil (1975), visiting professor at Columbia University (1976–1977), and research director at the École des Hautes Études en Sciences Sociales, in Paris (1982–1985). With the end of the dictatorship, he became Brazil's Ambassador to the European Economic Community (EEC) between 1985 and 1986 and Minister of Culture from 1986 to 1988. Then he was appointed member of several international commissions. He died on November 20, 2004 (Seccareccia & Correa 2014; d'Aguiar 2014; Kay 2005).

Like the heterodox economists who influenced him, Celso Furtado was in open rebellion during his career against the static, formalistic, and ahistorical approach of neoclassical economics, which he considered incapable of satisfactorily reflecting the economic realities of underdeveloped countries. It is, he said, a "trivial science, designed for people without imagination" (Furtado 1973: 33). The enigma he sought to solve throughout his career is why Brazil—and Latin America in general—is economically underdeveloped despite the abundant resources at its disposal. This stimulating quest gave rise to an impressive body of work— more than thirty books published in some fifteen languages—that helped to strengthen the structuralist current associated with ECLA and to cement his status as a pioneer of development economics (Szmrecsányi 2005; Kay 2005; Bielschowsky 2006; Mallorquin 2007; Boianovsky 2007, 2015, 2016; Fischer 2015).

Among the distinguishing features of structuralism are the theoretical choice to start from the global economic system as an analytical unit rather than from countries taken in isolation as well as the use of the historical-structural method as a means of identifying the socio-historical specificities of different social formations and of studying their interrelationships both diachronically and synchronically. Reformist in terms of economic policy, structuralists are critical of *laissez-faire*. They advocate an active intervention of the State posited as a central agent in the transformation of economic and social structures (Bielschowsky 2006; Boianovsky 2007, 2015, 2016).

Furtado's thinking was part of the high point of the Third World's intellectual revolt against the Western epistemic order—between the end of the Second World War and the mid-1970s: a period which is also that of "developmentalism." Latin American structuralism, of which he was a major theorist, constituted, together with the dependency research program, a kind of intellectual vanguard to the decolonization and national liberation movements that reconfigured world geopolitics in the mid-twentieth century. The Third World no longer wanted to be dissolved in the universalizing analyses coming from an "advanced" world that tends to project its own clichés and fantasies onto the rest of the world.

Starting from the analysis of Brazil's economic trajectory, Celso Furtado was led to address the question of the specificity of underdevelopment and the effects of the expansion of the capitalist system. According to him, the Industrial Revolution gave rise to two interdependent phenomena: development and under-development. Development and underdevelopment are Siamese twins created by the expansion of the capitalist system. Therefore, one cannot be conceived without the other. This utterly original thesis breaks both with evolutionary analyses à la Rostow (1960), which see underdevelopment as a stage preceding development, and with modernist perspectives, which rely on the diffusion of "modern" values and production techniques to propel underdeveloped countries onto the ramp of development. It also strikes down racist rationalizations of development gaps, alternately expressed in biological ("not the right skin color"), culturalist ("not the right culture") or pseudo-institutionalist ("not the right insti-tutions") terms. Furtado wrote:

> underdevelopment is an aspect of the way industrial capitalism has been growing and spreading from the beginning. [...] The study of underdevelopment must start with the identification of the particular types of structures created in the periphery of the capitalist economy by this system of international division of labor. Therefore, to build a model of an underdeveloped economy as a closed system is totally misleading. To isolate an underdeveloped economy from the general context of the expanding capitalist system is to dismiss from the beginning the fundamental problem of the nature of the external relation-ships of such an economy, namely the fact of its global dependence. (Furtado and Girvan 1973, p. 122)

According to Furtado, Brazil's peculiarity was that it industrialized—faster than other Third World countries—while still retaining the characteristics of underdevelopment. These are manifested through (1) large productivity gaps between urban and rural areas, (2) the increase in underemployed populations in urban areas, and (3) abyssal differences in living standards between a minority that concentrates a large part of the national income and a majority that lives at subsistence level. In a context—such as the Brazilian one—where the pace and direction of technical progress are dictated from outside, industrialization does not lead to a homogenization of production techniques and consumption patterns, especially if the distribution of income is very unequal. The rich minority tends to consume diversified goods whose production is capital-intensive, while the majority tends to consume poorly diversified goods produced with low technology.

What Furtado described as the Brazilian "model" in quotation marks, but which it would be more accurate to call the "Brazilian disease," refers to a situation of strong economic growth without "economic development." Indeed, between 1950 and 1982, Brazil's industrial sector grew by 8.1 percent annually, on average. While this exceptional growth rate increased the share of the industrial sector from 26 percent to 37 percent of GDP, it exacerbated income inequalities. The income share of the top 10 percent went from 39.7 percent in 1960 to 47.7 percent in 1980 (Baer 1986: 197–198; Barbosa 1998).

In Furtado's language, "economic development" is a concept synonymous with a wide social diffusion of the fruits of capital accumulation and technological innovation. He contrasted it with two other sources of economic growth: the exploitation/depletion of nonrenewable resources; and productivity gains resulting from insertion into the international division of labor. For him, Brazilian industrialization has been chiefly driven by the latter two sources, which tend to aggravate income inequalities. That's why its "most significant feature" is "its structural tendency to exclude the mass of the population from the benefits of accumulation and technical progress" (Furtado and Girvan 1973, p. 130).

These elements of analysis form the theoretical backdrop to *The Myth of Economic Development*.

Limits to Growth

The Myth of Economic Development is not among Celso Furtado's best-known books. In view of its radical conclusions this is certainly surprising. First published in Portuguese in 1974 under the title O *mito do desenvolvimento econômico* and translated into French two years later, the book is a lengthy discussion of *The Limits to Growth*, a landmark Club of Rome report that is worthy of some attention.

The Club of Rome was formed under the initiative of Aurelio Peccei, a businessman and humanist who was part of the Italian Resistance against fascism. The name of this network of friends comes from the fact that it met for the first time in 1968 in Rome. At that time, the aim of its distinguished members was to find solutions to what they called the "World Problematique," a broad concept referring to various problems associated with industrial civilization. In the list of the 66 "continuous critical problems" that the Club had identified, there were, for example, pollution, depletion of resources, malnutrition, poverty, war, racism, crime, terrorism, and so on. What are the links among all these problems? What is their common cause? How can they be solved? The Club of Rome commissioned a group of scientists including Donella Meadows,

Dennis Meadows, Jorgen Randers and William Behrens from the Massachusetts Institute of Technology (MIT) to work on these questions. Between 1970 and 1972, this research team developed a computer model based on the theory of system dynamics that allowed them to analyze the interrelationships and behavior between 1900 and 2100 of five main factors: population, industrial production, agricultural production, natural resources, and pollution. Their results were published in a book for the general public entitled *The Limits to Growth* (LTG).

LTG's major discovery was as explosive as it was counterintuitive. The main cause of the "world problematique," that is, the common denominator of the "continuous critical problems," is the pursuit of economic growth. In other words, if industrial civilization seems to be going wrong, and to be afflicted with many ills, the fault lies precisely with the "exponential growth of energy use, material flows and population against the earth's physical limits" (Meadows 2007: 193). This result was shocking to many because it was tantamount to saying "That which all the world sees as the solution to its problems is in fact a cause of those problems" (Meadows 1997: 193).

Why should economic growth be the source of humanity's problems when it is supposed to bring more prosperity for all? The reason for this is simple, according to the authors of LTG: in a world with finite / limited resources, infinite / unlimited growth is a logical and practical impossibility. The limits to economic growth are twofold. On the one hand, not all resources that allow exponential growth of capital, population, industry, and agriculture are renewable. Sooner or later, we reach limits on this side. On the other hand, the industrial system has irreversible consequences on the physical environment—including the atmosphere—which compromise the planet's ability to withstand the increased pressure it imposed on it.

Owing to the existence of such limits related to "sources" and "sinks," the pursuit of economic growth must necessarily lead to overshoot and then collapse, which will probably manifest itself in a sudden and uncontrollable decline in population and industrial capacity. Indeed, this is the most frequent result among the twelve scenarios modeled by the Meadows team. According to their projections, the limits of growth were to be reached within 100 years (that is, between 1970 and 2070), if the global trends observed in terms of population growth, industrialization, food production, pollution, and resource depletion were to continue. For the authors of LTG, this was not a prediction but rather a prognosis based on trends observed up to that point in time, which could be reversed were the political will to exist within the concert of nations.

Faced with the "techno-optimistic" belief that technological advances could push the limits of growth—for example, through more rational management of nonrenewable resources, the creation of substitutes, and a reduction in pollution levels—the authors of LTG were categorical. Technological advances will be needed to enable the transition to a new post-growth global economic system based on a new value system. But they will not be able to change the game. According to Meadows' team, changes in value system, especially in production, consumption, and reproduction patterns, will be much more decisive for the future of humanity than technological advances. Indeed, modern culture, which consists in "fighting against limits rather than learning to live with them," is part of the problem (Meadows et al., 1972: 150). Humanity must accept the need to live within the limits of the planet or face the prospect of a sudden collapse.

LTG's main recommendation was that nations must work quickly on the transition from Growth to Equilibrium. Being defined as the "non-growth state" or the state where population and capital at the world scale are constant, "Global Equilibrium" is not a state of mass impoverishment. It "could be designed so that the basic material needs of each person on earth are satisfied and each person has an equal opportunity to realize his individual human potential" (p. 24). The richest countries must be cooperative and agree to make significant adjustments in their lifestyles. For it is they who have unleashed the "growth syndrome" on humanity and who can materially afford to put an end to it. A global strategy is indispensable and it must include the underdeveloped countries whose particular needs should be taken into account.

LTG became a worldwide best-seller translated into some thirty languages, and one of the reference books in environmentalist literature. As soon as it was published, it had ardent supporters, but also fierce opponents, who were often recruited from conventional economists who did not want to be deprived of their professional *raison d'être*—propagating the "growthist" faith (Ketcham 2018). Unlike them, Celso Furtado had a more constructive engagement with LTG. He immediately recognized it as an original work because for the first time researchers had modeled the world economy as a closed system. Until then, the dominant approach had been to start from individual countries and assume that nonrenewable resources were unlimited in the "outside world"—that is, the rest of the world. He also stressed its importance: LTG addressed an overarching issue largely ignored by economists, namely, the consequences of capital accumulation for the physical environment.

While praising LTG's approach and reach, Celso Furtado criticized it for obscuring the great dependence of central countries on the natural resources of the peripheral countries. This is, however, a relatively minor criticism. For his fundamental criticism is that LTG made projections based on a questionable, not to say disproved, assumption: "as the rest of the world develops economically, it will follow basically the U.S. pattern of consumption" (Meadows et al., 1972: 109).

In *The Myth of Economic Development*, Furtado explained from a structuralist perspective why the hypothesis that the consumption style of the countries of the center could be generalized to the rest of humanity betrays an ignorance of the specificity of underdevelopment and, consequently, why it is flawed. He concluded his discussion by indicating the main conclusions that Third World countries should, in his view, draw from LTG.

A structuralist reading of LTG

Furtado distinguishes three phases in the evolution of industrial capitalism. The first corresponded to the Industrial Revolution and the construction of British hegemony. The second marked the contestation of the latter by countries that were to build *national economic systems*: that is, to acquire a nationally integrated and articulated industrial structure that favors greater homogeneity in production techniques and consumption patterns. These countries would subsequently form the center of the world economic system—the United States, Western Europe, and Japan.

The third phase began in the middle of the 20th century. It corresponded to the experience of the countries in the periphery, mostly former colonies or dependent territories that were integrated into the capitalist system during the first phase as exporters of raw materials and importers of manufactured goods. Having since then maintained this specialization, these countries have not had the opportunity to set up national economic systems. This is why, unlike the central countries, their industrialization initially took the form of *import-substitution industrialization*. Another historical peculiarity is that industrialization in the periphery was stimulated by the activity of the multinationals in the center. For it took place in a context where the greater integration between the central countries had been a favorable breeding ground for the emergence of multinationals and the deployment of their activities on a global scale. When they operate in the periphery, they can overcome the traditional obstacles to industrialization linked to the small size of domestic markets, the lack of capital, and the low level of technological development.

According to Furtado, industrialization in the periphery of the capitalist system has different properties from that in the center. In the latter case, it is accompanied by an increase in wages in line with that of productivity and stability in the income distribution. This encourages an extension of domestic markets, the diffusion of new goods and services, and a homogenization of consumption patterns. On the other hand, in the periphery, industrialization is driven more by the dynamism of the export-oriented sectors controlled by the multinationals from the center than by the internal process of capital accumulation and technological innovation. The result is both technological heterogeneity—the coexistence of a "modern" sector with the "traditional" economy—and social heterogeneity—significant income inequalities between a minority that operates in the "modern" sector and tries to imitate the way of life of the central countries, on the one hand, and the vast majority that lives at subsistence level with a poorly diversified basket of consumer goods that require relatively little capital for their production, on the other. Consequently, the faster industrialization accelerates, the more it tends to worsen income distribution and thus maintain the structures of underdevelopment. Furtado summarized the differences between central and peripheral industrialization by arguing that they correspond to two distinct modes of allocation of the *economic surplus*. In the central countries, the latter is invested in productive activities, whereas in the peripheral countries it tends to feed imports, especially those of interest to the privileged minority anxious to imitate the consumption patterns of the developed countries.

Just as the second phase of the evolution of industrial capitalism resulted in a greater *centralization of economic decisions* compared to the first, the third phase went even further in this area compared to the second—with the important difference that it was now the monopolies (the term used in Marxist literature to designate oligopolies / large multinational companies) more than the states that constituted the centers of economic decision-making. The functions of the state changed accordingly in the center and in the periphery. With regard to the countries of the center, Furtado had a rather positive appreciation of the role of monopolies: "Favoring innovation in all of its forms, the oligopoly constitutes a powerful instrument in economic expansion" (p. 16). Thanks to their greater coordination of economic activity, "the human and social costs of the operation of capitalist economies have been considerably reduced" (p. 36). This view is the exact opposite of that of Baran and Sweezy (1966), for whom the era of monopoly capitalism is synonymous with irrationality, waste, choking of innovation, and ultimately economic stagnation. In peripheral countries, Furtado observed that monopolies have two contradictory effects on the state apparatus. On the one hand, they contribute to modernizing the bureaucracy by inducing it to be more efficient in carrying out the tasks they expect from it. On the other hand, they consecrate the impotence of the state, which is no longer able to *direct* and *coordinate* economic activity. As long as this is the case, as long as economic decisions remain in the hands of monopolies, the most "advanced" peripheral countries will not be able to emerge from a socially polarizing type of accumulation. Indeed, monopolies are not interested in another *economic orientation* in the periphery—for example, a more egalitarian type of accumulation.

Thus, according to Furtado, the functioning of the world economic system since the Industrial Revolution has structurally contributed to increasing income inequalities between the center and the periphery, but also within the periphery. This trend has been exacerbated rather than slowed down in the era of monopoly capitalism. Therefore, Furtado stressed, the hypothesis that the standard of living of people in the periphery will converge toward that of the rich countries must be rejected. This led him to three conclusions.

First, the pressure on natural resources in the future will be much less than that projected by LTG, since the consumption pattern of the central countries concerns only a minority of the world's population and can never be generalized to the whole planet. The "cataclysm" scenario, that of the collapse of industrial civilization, therefore seemed unlikely to him "on a foreseeable horizon":

> the predominant evolutionary tendency is to exclude nine out of ten people from the principal benefits of development; and, if we observe the group of peripheral countries in particular, we realize that there the tendency is to exclude nineteen out of twenty. This growing mass of the excluded—in absolute and relative terms—that is concentrated in peripheral countries constitutes in itself a heavy factor in the evolution of the system (p. 55).

Second, Furtado continued, in the light of the polarizing trend of industrial capitalism, the results highlighted by LTG should be interpreted differently. Indeed, according to him, the merit of this scientific work is that it has shown *incidentally* that the generalization of the Western way of life must lead to the collapse of civilization.

> [LTG] provides a thorough demonstration that the lifestyle created by industrial capitalism will always be the privilege of a minority. The cost of this lifestyle, in terms of the degradation of the physical world, is so high that any attempt to generalize it would inevitably lead to the collapse of an entire civilization, putting the survival of the human species at risk. We have then thorough evidence that *economic development*—the idea that the *poor peoples* can one day enjoy the lifestyles of the currently *rich peoples*—is simply unattainable. We now know incontrovertibly that peripheral economies will never be developed, in the sense of being similar to the economies that currently make up the center of the capitalist system (p. 56).

The "economic development" that the Third World countries are promised is therefore a "myth" in the sense of an illusion because it can never take place and in any case the central countries have no interest in it (Furtado 1974: 64). For, otherwise, how could they afford a way of life characterized by an ill-considered waste of the planet's resources? Economic development is also a myth in the sense of a functional ideology: it justifies the status quo by legitimizing the maintenance of the system of industrial capitalism, as well as its destructions on the cultural and environmental planes.

Finally, starting from the observation that industrial capitalism has nothing to offer as a prospect of a decent life for the vast majority of humanity, Furtado outlined the principles of an alternative *orientation of development* that should be more egalitarian and more economical in resources. To that end, priority should be given to a wide social dissemination of consumer products whose production escapes the modernist cult of planned obsolescence.

An enduring myth

Despite its publication 46 years ago, and the important changes that have taken place in the meantime, the message of *The Myth of Economic Development* is still highly topical. Today, climate change, and in particular global warming, is the specter that haunts the survival of the human species. According to the *Living Planet 2018* report,

> In the last 50 years, global average temperature has risen at 170 times the background rate. Ocean acidification may be occurring at a rate not seen in at least 300 million years. Earth is losing biodiversity at a rate seen only during mass extinctions. And still more change may be headed our way

as people are responsible for releasing 100 billion tonnes of carbon into the Earth system every 10 years (WWF 2018: 23).

To reflect these dramatic changes, the concept of the "Anthropocene" has been advanced to describe a new geological era characterized by the significant influence of human action on the physical environment. Even more suggestively, the "Capitalocene" concept has been proposed to link environmental degradation with the unbridled logic of capital accumulation (Moore 2016).

Celso Furtado did not see such a development coming. For he did, somehow, underestimate the significance of the Club of Rome report—the results of which were not subsequently contradicted by the global models that carried out the same exercise (Meadows 2007: 195). His claim that LTG's "catastrophic conclusions" should be rejected was not entirely justified. In fact, his focus was on trends in nonrenewable resources. He did not really address the question of the impact of the industrial civilization, from its origins until then, on the carrying capacity—the biocapacity—of the Earth. Indeed, even if economic growth may not be limited by the availability of natural resources for a long time to come, as he argued, it may be limited by the saturation of the "sinks." What currently endangers the survival of humanity is less the exhaustion of "sources" than the diminishing capacity of the planet to bear the irreversible damage inflicted by the pursuit of economic growth.

In any case, the particularly ecocidal character of the Capitalocene reinforces, and in no way invalidates, Furtado's other two conclusions—that economic development is a myth and that the countries of the Global South in particular—and humanity in general—must find an alternative model to the capitalist system and not only to "industrial capitalism." In view of the tenacious belief that economic growth is the solution to contemporary problems, including climate change, his conclusions still deserve to be strongly reiterated.

Indeed, the idea that the countries of the global South can catch up with the standard of living of the developed countries stems from a truncated reading of the latter's economic trajectory. In Europe, in particular, industrialization in the nineteenth century certainly made it possible to absorb a large part of the labor force released by the agriculture and crafts sectors. But it was not enough to absorb the surplus labor force. Emigration, especially to the Americas, provided the main outlet. However, if the countries of the Global South are to follow the same development trajectory, this must lead to a large dispossession of peasants and thus to the creation of a large surplus labor force. The latter would not be absorbed by the "modern" sector, due to the absence of industries or to the capital-intensive nature of the technologies used. Under these conditions, in the absence of new "available" Americas somewhere on the planet, disparity in living conditions must remain the norm, as currently observed in most countries of the Global South. As Samir Amin explained:

> the development of capitalism in Europe, the United States and in Japan reduced the active population engaged in agriculture to 5 per cent in each of its regions, without compromising the capacity of the new capitalist modernized agriculture to meet demands for expanded food production. Why then should it not be possible for the countries of the periphery to be set on an accelerated course down this same path—even if somewhat belatedly? This proposition is unsustainable because it

ignores the specific conditions which allowed the West to prosper and which, in themselves, preclude their own reproduction elsewhere. Its success, for instance, was only made possible because the industries established at the time, during the nineteenth century, were able to absorb a large proportion of rural populations expelled from the countryside. In addition, surplus populations had the option of mass migration to the Americas (considering that the European population made up 15 per cent of the world's population in the 1500s and that combined with the European descendants in America, it made up 36 per cent of the population in 1900, emigration abroad allowed for the development of a "second Europe"). In the contemporary situation, the demands that industries in the peripheries should be "competitive" on world markets justify the use of modern technologies which reduce the level of labour-intensive work. At the same time, there are no new Americas to open for mass migrations from Asia or Africa. In such conditions, the pursuit of a model based on historical capitalism produces nothing other than migration from devastated countrysides to squalid urban slums (2017: 3).

The limited opportunities for large-scale emigration to newer "Americas" is an important reason why the countries of the Global South cannot replicate the development trajectory of the West. Another no less important reason is that from the beginnings of capitalism until today the economic development of the West has been based on the capture of the biocapacity of the countries of the Global South. The conquest of the Americas has been one of the major ecocides of the modern period (Sale 2006: 81–82). Today, 2.8 planets would be needed if all the inhabitants of the earth had the same ecological footprint as the average resident of the European Union. The EU represents only 7 percent of the world's population yet uses 20 percent of the planet's biocapacity (WWF 2019). The "ecological imperialism" of rich countries, expressed in part as "unequal ecological exchange," consists of keeping poorer countries in a situation where they cannot afford to rationally exploit their resources for their own internal consumption (Patnaik and Patnaik 2017) and making them bear the ecological costs of capitalist expansion (Givens et al. 2019; Foster and Holleman 2014). This trend has become more evident in the neoliberal era marked by the "financialization" of capitalism (Frame 2016).

In line with Celso Furtado's predictions, economic inequalities between developed countries and the Global South have worsened. For most of the latter, the dominant long-term trend has not been economic catch-up—the generalization of the Western way of life—but rather social polarization accompanied by significant environmental degradation. This is true even for China and India despite the spectacular progress they have both made in the meantime (Milanovic 2012: 100–103). The case of China, the world's largest polluter in absolute terms but far behind Western countries in relative terms, is also interesting in that it eloquently illustrates Furtado's proposition that any attempt to universalize the Western way of life risks accelerating collapse. It is estimated that global electricity and car production would have both to increase 14-fold if the average Chinese person were to have the same level of consumption as the average American (Goldstein and Lemoine 2013: 94). Air pollution is also believed to be responsible for 1.6 million premature deaths each year in China (Stanway 2017).

Within the countries of the Global South, economic inequalities seem to have increased; when they have decreased, as in the case of Brazil, they remain at very high levels. On this point too, Furtado was right. However, the Brazilian economist had not anticipated the increase in income and wealth inequalities within developed countries where, over the last four decades, real wages for the vast majority of workers have more or less stagnated despite the increase in labor productivity. This has led to greater income concentration and a declining trend in the share of labor in national income (Piketty 2014). The advent of "financial capitalism" has thus meant that it is no longer only in the periphery that growing masses are excluded from the fruits of capital accumulation and technical progress. This trend inherent to capitalism no longer spares the countries of the center. And it is associated with increased pressure on nonrenewable resources. In other words, for a growing proportion of citizens in rich countries, economic development has also become a myth.

On the occasion of the 100th anniversary of Celso Furtado's birth, we should greatly welcome the publication in English of a book whose message will continue to resonate and challenge us all as long as the countries of the North persist in defending economic growth and the countries of the South remain blinded by the illusory promise of economic catch-up.

—Ndongo Samba Sylla

References

d'Aguiar, Rosa Freire (2014) "Celso Furtado: The Struggles of an Economist," *International Journal of Political Economy* 43(4): 7–14.

Amin, Samir (2017) "Tribute to Sam Moyo," *Agrarian South: Journal of Political Economy* 5(2 & 3): 1–20.

Baer, Werner (1986) "Growth with Inequality: The Cases of Brazil and Mexico," *Latin American Research Review* 21(2): 197–207.

Baran, Paul A. and Paul M. Sweezy (1966) *Monopoly Capital: An Essay on the American Economic and Social Order.* New York: Monthly Review Press.

Barbosa, Fernando de Holanda (1998) "Economic Development: the Brazilian Experience." In A. Hosono, N. Saavedra-Rivano, eds. *Development Strategies in East Asia and Latin America.* London: Palgrave Macmillan, 69–87.

Bielschowsky, Ricardo (2006) "Celso Furtado's Contributions to Structuralism and Their Relevance Today," *Cepal Review* 8(8), April: 7–14.

Boianovsky, Mauro (2016) "The Structuralist Research Program in Development Economics." In Claudia Sunna and Davide Gualerzi, eds. *Development Economics in the 21st Century.* London and New York: Routledge, 88–103.

———(2015) "Between Lévi-Strauss and Braudel: Furtado and the Historical-Structural Method in Latin American Political Economy," *Journal of Economic Methodology* 22(4): 413–438.

———(2007). "A View from the Tropics: Celso Furtado and the Theory of Economic Development in the 1950s," *History of Political Economy* 42(2): 221–266.

Fischer, Andrew A. (2015) "The End of Peripheries? On the Enduring Relevance of Structuralism for Understanding Contemporary Global Development," *Development and Change* 46(4): 700–732.

Foster, John Bellamy, and Hannah Holleman (2014) "The Theory of Unequal Ecological Exchange: A Marx-Odum Dialectic," *The Journal of Peasant Studies* 41(2): 199–233.

Frame, Mariko Lin (2016) "The Neoliberalization of (African) Nature as the Current Phase of Ecological Imperialism," *Capitalism Nature Socialism* 27(1): 1–19.

Furtado, Celso (1972) "Sous-développement, dépendance: une hypothèse globale," *Tiers-Monde* 13(52): 697–702.

———(1973) "Adventures of a Brazilian Economist," *International Social Science Journal* 45(1/2): 28–38, UNESCO, Paris.

———(1974) "Le mythe du développement et le futur du Tiers Monde," *Revue Tiers Monde* 15(57): 57–68.

Furtado, Celso and Cherita Girvan (1973) "The Brazilian 'Model,'" *Social and Economic Studies* 22(1): 122–131.

Givens, Jennifer E., Xiaorui Huang, and Andrew K. Jorgenson (2019) "Ecologically Unequal Exchange: A Theory of Global Environmental *In*justice," *Sociology Compass* 13(5).

Goldstein, Andrea, and Françoise Lemoine (2013) *L'économie des BRIC (Brésil, Russie, Inde, Chine).* Paris: La Découverte.

Kay, Cristobal (2005) "Celso Furtado: Pioneer of Structuralist Development Theory," *Development and Change* 36(6): 1201–1207.

Ketcham, Christopher (2018) "The Fallacy of Endless Economic Growth. What Economists Around the World Get Wrong About the Future," *Pacific Standard*, 22 September.

Mallorquín, Carlos (2007) "Celso Furtado and Development: An Outline," *Development in Practice* 17(6): 807–819.

Meadows, Donella H. (2007) "The history and conclusions of *The Limits to Growth*," *System Dynamics Review* 23(2/3): 191–197.

Meadows, Donella H., Dennis L. Meadows, and Jorgen Randers (2000) *Limits to Growth. The 30-Year Update.* London and Sterling, VA: Earthscan.

Meadows, Donella H., Dennis L. Meadows, Jorgen Randers, and William W. Behrens III (1972) *The Limits to Growth: A Report for the Club of Rome's Project on the Predicament of Mankind.* New York: Universe Books.

Milanovic, Branko (2012) *The Haves and the Have-Nots. A Brief and Idiosyncratic History of Global Inequality.* New York: Basic Books.

Moore, Jason W., ed. (2016) *Anthropocene or Capitalocene? Nature, History, and the Crisis of Capitalism.* Oakland, CA: PM Press.

Patnaik, Utsa, and Prabhat Patnaik (2017) *A Theory of Imperialism.* New York: Columbia University Press.

Piketty, Thomas (2014) *Capital in the Twenty-first Century.* Oxford: Belknap Press.

Rostow, Walt W. (1960) *The Stages of Economic Growth: A Non-Communist Manifesto.* Cambridge: Cambridge University Press.

Sale, Kirkpatrick (2006) *Christopher Columbus and the Conquest of Paradise.* London: Tauris Parke Paperbacks.

Seccareccia, Mario, and Eugenia Correa (2014) "Celso Furtado and Development Theory," *International Journal of Political Economy* 43(4): 3–6.

Stanway, David (2017) "China Cuts Smog but Health Damage Already Done: Study," Reuters, 17 April.

Szmrecsányi, Tamás (2005) "The Contributions of Celso Furtado (1920–2004) to Development Economics," *The European Journal of the History of Economic Thought* 12(4): 689–700.

WWF (2018) *Living Planet Report—2018: Aiming*

Higher. Grooten, M. and Almond, R.E.A., eds. Gland, Switzerland: WWF.

————(2019) *EU Overshoot Day Report. Living Beyond Nature's Limits*. Brussels, Belgium.

1

The Prophecy of Collapse

Myths have exercised an undeniable influence over the minds of men who endeavor to understand social reality. From the *bon sauvage* Rousseau dreamed of, to Marx's millenary idea of the disappearance of the State, from Malthus's "populational principle" to the Walrasian concept of general equilibrium, social scientists have always sought support in some hypothesis rooted in a system of values that they rarely make explicit. Myth gathers a group of hypotheses that cannot be tested. This is no great problem, however, because analytical work is performed at a level much closer to reality. The principal function of myth is to orient, on an intuitive plane, the construction of what Schumpeter called the *vision* of the social process, without which analytical work would have no meaning whatsoever. In this way, myths function as lighthouses that illuminate the perceptual field of the social scientist, allowing him to have a clear vision of certain problems and to see nothing of others. At the same time, they provide intellectual comfort, because the evaluative distinctions he draws arise in his spirit as a *reflection* of objective reality.[1]

The literature concerning economic development from the past quarter-century gives us an excellent example of the guiding role of myths in the social sciences: at least 90 percent of what we encounter there is founded on the idea (taken as a given) that *economic development*, as it has been practiced by the countries that led the Industrial Revolution, can be universalized. Or, more precisely: they pretend that the standards of consumption found in the minority of humanity, which currently lives in highly industrialized countries, are accessible to the great population masses in rapid expansion that form the so-called Third World. This idea certainly constitutes a prolonging of the myth of *progress*, an essential element in the directing ideology of the bourgeois revolution from which the current industrial society was created.

With the perception of reality narrowed by this guiding concept, economists began to devote the best parts of their intellect to conceiving complex schemes of the process of capital accumulation in which the dynamic impulse is produced by technological advances, an entelechy conceived outside any social context. Little to no attention was given to the cultural consequences of the exponential growth of capital stock. The great modern metropoles—with their unbreathable air, growing criminality, deterioration of public services, and escape of youth through counterculture—arose as a nightmare in the dream of linear progress in which theoreticians of growth nestled. Even less attention was given to the impact on the physical environment of a system of decisions whose ultimate objectives are to satisfy private interests. This is the origin of the irritation caused among many economists by the study

The Limits to Growth, prepared by an interdisciplinary group at MIT, for the so-called Club of Rome.[2] It is not necessary to agree with all the methodological aspects of this study—and even less so with its conclusions—to recognize its fundamental importance. This study brought to the forefront of discussion crucial problems that economists of economic development have always tried to leave in the shadows. For the first time we are equipped with a set of representative data on fundamental aspects of the structure and general tendencies of what is beginning to be called the planetary economic system. Furthermore, we are equipped with a body of information that allows us to formulate some background questions related to the future of the so-called "underdeveloped" countries.

In truth, the practice of constructing representative models of the structure and short-term functioning of large sectors of economic activities is not new. Two centuries passed between the *tableau économique* of the French physiocrats and the Leontief matrices, during which we learned something about the interdependence of economic activities. In the last quarter-century, complex models of national economies have been developed—those that are relatively small but very open to the outside world, like Holland's, or those that are larger and more self-centered, like that of the United States. The analytical knowledge provided by these models has allowed for the formulation of hypotheses about the more long-term behavior of certain variables, particularly the demand for products the United States government considers to be of strategic value. These studies brought to light the fact that the U.S. economy tends to be increasingly *dependent* on nonrenewable resources produced outside the country.[3] This is undoubtedly a conclusion of great importance—one that is at the root of the United States economy's policy of growing *openness* and of strengthening large companies capable of promoting the exploitation of natural resources on a global scale. The more long-term projections, done at the analytical level to which we have just referred, are implicitly based on the idea that the outer confines of this system are limitless.[4] The concept of dynamic reserves, a function of the volume of scheduled investments and of hypotheses about the progress of technology, serves to calm the most inquisitive spirits. Because policies for the protection of nonrenewable resources are up to governments and not the companies that exploit them—and because the information (and the capacity to comprehend it) lies primarily with the companies—the problem tends to be lost to view.

The importance of the study done for the Club of Rome derives precisely from the fact that it abandoned the hypothesis of an open system with regard to the limits of natural resources. In it there is no trace of concern about the growing *dependence* of highly industrialized countries on the natural resources of other countries, and even less worry about the consequences for the latter of the predatory use of these resources by the former. Their breakthrough is that they succeeded in closing the system on a planetary level, in an initial estimation of nonrenewable resources.[5] Once the system was closed, the authors of the study asked themselves the following question: what will happen if the *economic development*, toward which all peoples of the earth are being mobilized, actually materializes—that is, what if the current lifestyles of the rich actually become universal? The answer to this question is clear and unambiguous: if this were to happen, the pressure on nonrenewable resources and the pollution of the environment would reach such a scale (or, alternatively, the cost of controlling pollution would be so high) that the global economic system would necessarily collapse.

Before considering what real significance we should attribute to this prophecy, we ought to consider a more general problem that modern man has attempted to elude. I speak of the predatory nature of the process of civilization, particularly the variant of this process engendered by the Industrial Revolution. We cannot overlook the evidence that in our civilization the creation of economic *value*, in the vast majority of cases, sets in motion irreversible processes of degradation to the physical world. The economist limits his observational scope to partial processes, pretending not to see that these processes cause growing changes in the physical world.[6] The majority of them transform free or available energy, over which man has total control, into unavailable energy. Aside from its overtly economic consequences, this process causes a rise in the average temperature of certain areas of the planet, the consequences of which—on a longer-term basis—can hardly be overstated. The naïve attitude consists of imagining that problems of this magnitude will inevitably be solved by technological advances, as if the current acceleration of technological progress were not contributing to the aggravation of these problems. This is not about speculating as to whether science and technology *theoretically* allow man to solve this or that problem created by our civilization. This is simply about recognizing that what we call the *economic value added* has as its counterpart irreversible processes in the physical world, the consequences of which we try to ignore. It is important not to forget that in industrial civilization, the future is in large part conditioned by the decisions that have already been made in the past and/or those that are being made in the present based on short-term priorities. The more capital accumulation advances, the greater the interdependence between the future and the past. Consequently, the inertia of the system grows, and course corrections become slower or require more effort.

2

The Structural Evolution of the Capitalist System

Conjectures about the fate of our civilization, fascinating though they may occasionally appear, have a minimal impact on the spirit of the common man. Human psychology is such that we can rarely concentrate for long on problems that extend beyond a relatively short time horizon. My objective is more limited and precise and can be synthesized in a simple question: in the face of the present tendencies of the capitalist system, what options are available to the countries who were subjected to the deformation of underdevelopment? From which point of view can the study we referred to earlier be useful in this exploration of the future?

From the start, we must recognize the unrealistic nature of the model used to project the world economy and, consequently, the irrelevance of the catastrophic conclusions presented. How can we allow a model, based on the observation of the historic behavior of currently industrialized economies and on their present structure, to be used to project the long-term tendencies of the process of industrialization on a global scale?

Indeed, the structure of this model is founded on the strict observation of the bloc of economies that led the process of industrialization, that were able to utilize the most easily accessible natural resources, and that gained control over a large part of the nonrenewable resources found in underdeveloped countries.[1] We are not talking about a methodological simplification, an initial estimate to be corrected when additional information is available. Simply put, we are talking about a structure that reflects an inadequate observation of reality and is therefore unsuitable for projecting any of its tendencies.

The question that immediately comes to mind is the following: do we have enough knowledge of the global economy's structure (or, rather, of the aggregate of capitalist economies) to project its significant long-term tendencies? Even though we may not be willing to give an unequivocal affirmative answer to this question, we cannot fail to recognize that there is ample information about the process of industrialization in countries with various degrees of economic development. Because we have access to this information, it is no longer possible to accept the claim, espoused by the authors of this study, according to which "as the rest of the world develops economically, it will follow basically the U.S. pattern of consumption."[2] The acceptance of this doctrine implies ignoring the specificity of the phenomenon of underdevelopment. It is to this doctrine that we owe the confusion between an underdeveloped economy and a "young country"; it is to this doctrine that we owe the conception of development as a sequence of unavoidable phases, à la Rostow.[3]

Capturing the nature of underdevelopment is no easy task: it has many dimensions, and those that are easily visible are not always the most significant. But if we know something for certain it is that underdevelopment has nothing to do with the age of a society or of a country. And we also know that the criteria for measuring it are the degree of capital accumulation applied to productive processes and the degree of access to the arsenal of consumer goods characterizing what is now commonly dubbed the modern lifestyle. It is clear even to the superficial observer that underdevelopment is linked to greater technological heterogeneity, which reflects the nature of the external relations of this type of economy.

When we take a panoramic view of the global economy over the course of the 19th century, particularly during its second half, we see that the enormous transformations that occurred revolved around two processes: the first refers to a considerable acceleration in capital accumulation in production systems, and the second, to an equally considerable intensification of international commerce. Both processes generated substantial increases in the productivity of the workforce, giving birth to a growing surplus that would be used to intensify accumulation even more and to finance the expansion and diversification of private and public consumption. How this surplus was appropriated and how its use was oriented constitute the fundamental problem in the study of the evolution of industrial capitalism and its process of maturing. During an initial phase, a large part of the surplus mentioned above was channeled to Great Britain, transforming London into the financial nerve center of the capitalist world. Financing infrastructural investments in the entire world on behalf of the interests of international commerce, Great Britain promoted and consolidated the implantation of a system of international division of labor that would indelibly mark the evolution of industrial capitalism. This system favored the geographic concentration of the capital accumulation process due to the simple fact that, because of external economies and economies of scale, industrial activities—which represented the sector with most rapidly expanding demand—tended to cluster together.

The reaction against the British global economic project soon manifested itself. The second phase of the evolution of industrial capitalism was marked by this reaction: it was the period of consolidation of the *national economic systems* of countries that would make up the developed economies club in the current century. The way in which this awareness emerged is a fascinating chapter of modern history, but it is one that lies beyond our immediate interest. It is enough to emphasize that, all over the world, the success of this reaction was linked to a much greater centralization of economic decision-making than that which had existed during the consolidation phase of British industrial capitalism. In some places, this greater centralization would be achieved through the preeminence of the banking system, which would undergo an important structural evolution; in others, the nation-state took a greater role in directing the process of accumulation.[4] In all quarters, this orientation led to alliances between social classes and groups—industrial, commercial, and financial bourgeoisies; rural landowners; the state bureaucracy—around a "national project," with significant repercussions in the evolution of industrial capitalism. And while, in the British phase, international commerce grew more quickly than production in the system's center, the tendency would now be the opposite.[5] The evolution of the terms of trade tended to be unfavorable for the system's periphery—that is, for countries who provided raw materials. Meanwhile, accumulation continued to be concentrated in the center, now transformed into a group of countries with varying degrees of industrialization. On the other hand, the new shape capitalism took—greater centralization of decisions at the national level—facilitated the concentration of economic power and the emergence of large companies. International markets began to be controlled by groups of companies, cartelized to varying degrees.[6]

Why this country and not that one crossed the demarcation line and joined the developed countries club in this second crucial phase of the evolution of industrial capitalism (situated between the 1870s and the First World War) is a problem whose answer belongs more to history than to economic analysis. Nowhere did this crossing occur within the framework of *laissez-faire*: it was always the result of a policy conceived deliberately to that end. What is important to highlight is that the demarcation line gradually became more entrenched. Because industrialization in each era is shaped according to the degree of accumulation attained by the countries that lead the process, the relative effort required to take the first steps tends to increase over time. What is more, once the relative delay reaches a certain point, the process of industrialization undergoes important qualitative modifications. It is no longer oriented to form a national economic system, but rather to complete the international economic system. Some industries arise integrated with certain export activities, and others as complements to import activities. In one way or another, they amplify their degree of integration in the international economic system. During periods of crisis for this system, they seek to reduce the amount of imports of certain industrial activities, which occasionally leads to the installation of industries that integrate the economic system at a national level. In this way, through a reverse process—by means of an effort to reduce the instability resulting from how it was inserted into the international economy—an industrial system with a greater or lesser degree of integration is formed.

It is worth noting that this industrial system, formed around a market previously supplied from abroad and generated by the process of "import substitution,"[7] is specific to underdeveloped economies. It demonstrates unique characteristics that should be taken into account in any attempt to make projections about the whole of the global economy. To understand what is unique to this new type of industrialization, we must take a few steps back and reflect on the situation of those economic subgroups that were integrated into the international capitalist system during the phase of British hegemony, and which continued to be exporters of primary products in the subsequent phase of expansion of the system's center. In these economies, the increases in productivity fundamentally resulted from the expansion of exports and not from the process of accumulation and the technological advances that accompanied this accumulation in the system's center. It was a question of incorporating underutilized or recently acquired productive resources, as in the case of immigrant labor, into a productive system that was growing horizontally. These increases in productivity resulted from what, since Ricardo, we in economics have called "comparative advantages." The liberal doctrine, through which the English justified their project of international division of labor with such conviction, relied on this *law* of comparative advantages.

That countries—with their abundance of unused lands and the possibility of receiving immigrants (or of using more intensely a workforce incorporated into a precapitalist system)—opted for the path of least resistance of comparative advantages is not surprising. After all, Great Britain was also opting for comparative advantages when it drastically reduced its agriculture and concentrated on industry and even on the production of coal, part of which it exported. What creates the fundamental difference and brings about the dividing line between development and underdevelopment is the orientation toward utilizing the surplus generated by the increase in productivity. Industrial activity tends to concentrate a large part of the surplus in a few hands and to keep it under the control of the social group directly committed to the productive process. On the other hand, because the capital invested in industry is constantly being renewed, the door remains permanently open to the introduction of innovations. In this way, an industrial system tends to sustain its own growth, unless it is subjected to a lack of effective demand. This explains why, in the second phase of the evolution of industrial capitalism, those countries that sought to create a national economic system protected agricultural and other activities that did not offer "comparative advantages." Through this protection they guaranteed demand to the industrial sector, generously compensating for what they lost in other "protected" activities with productivity increases in this sector.

In the countries in which comparative advantages take the shape of specialization in exporting primary products (particularly agricultural products), the additional surplus takes the form of an increase in imports. Because specialization does not require or imply modifications to the methods of production, and because accumulation happens with local resources (the opening of lands, roads and rural constructions, the growth of flocks, etc.),[8] the increase in the capacity to import remains available for use in the acquisition of consumer goods. In this way, it is through demand for finished consumer goods that these countries insert themselves more deeply into industrial civilization. This fact is fundamental to understanding the importance that the process of industrialization will assume in a subsequent phase. My intention here is not to address in detail the problems specific to so-called import substitution industrialization. I will limit myself to emphasizing that it tends to replicate, on a miniature scale, industrial systems supported by a much broader process of capital accumulation. In practice, this replication in miniature happens when companies from core countries install their subsidiaries in the country in question, which reinforces the tendency to reproduce patterns of consumption found in societies with a much higher level of average income. The result is the familiar syndrome of a tendency toward income concentration, so familiar to all who study the industrialization of underdeveloped countries.

The rapid industrialization of the capitalist world's periphery under the direction of companies from core countries, which we have observed since the Second World War, corresponds to a third phase in the evolution of industrial capitalism. This phase began with a process of integrating the national economies that make up the system's center. From the drafting of the Havana Charter and the creation of the GATT to the Kennedy Round, moving on to the formation of the European Single Market,[9] considerable steps were taken toward structuring a unified economic space in the center of the capitalist system. Within this space in the process of unification, the movement of capital grew to a considerable volume (primarily from the United States toward Western Europe, but also, in a more recent phase, in the opposite direction). This allowed large companies to implant themselves in all national subsystems and also allowed oligopolistic structures to encompass the whole of these subsystems. Beginning in the second half of the 1960s, the formation of an important international capital market constituted the crowning event of this process, because it permitted large companies to free themselves of many of the limitations created by national monetary and financial systems.[10]

In this way, national systems—which in the previous phase had been the boundary markers of the industrialization process—gradually lost their individuality in the center of the capitalist system, without the clear appearance of another marker to replace them. The tendency was to create a situation somewhat similar to that which prevailed during the time Great Britain was the sole center of the capitalist system. In the same way in which the English entrepreneur, who financed his project in the City, felt free to locate his activity in any part of the world, the "international" partner of an American or Italian company managed from Luxembourg or Switzerland also felt free to begin or to expand its activities in this or that country, financing its operations in whatever way it saw fit, based on its own goals of expansion. What distinguishes this from the old British model is that the individual entrepreneur has been substituted by the large company.

Though we find similarities to the old British system, it is important to recognize that the similarities to the capitalism of the national systems consolidation phase are also significant. Indeed, it was in the sphere of the latter that the large company assumed the role of decision-making center capable of influencing important sectors of economic activities. The large company requires a much more advanced degree of coordination in economic decisions than that which corresponds to atomized markets. This greater coordination was initially reached through the tutelage of the banking system or directly from government organs.[11] But, as large companies matured and availed themselves of professional directors, they began to develop rules of coexistence that allowed for the exchange of a minimum of necessary information to assure a certain level of coordination in decisions. This evolution occurred initially in the United States, where the great depth of experience allowed them to explore multiple possibilities. The tendency toward concentration, which created situations of virtual monopoly in certain branches, generated opposition in defense of the public interest, such as the antitrust laws of the end of the 19th century. Once the door to monopoly was closed, it was necessary to develop more subtle forms of coordination. The oligopoly represents the pinnacle of this evolution: it permits a small group of large firms to create barriers to entry for others in a given sector of economic activity, and to jointly control the prices of certain products while still preserving financial, technological, and administrative autonomy. Controlling prices creates a relative advantage for the companies that are the most innovative in both productive processes and the introduction of new products into a given sector. In contrast to traditional price competition—which translates into a reduction of profits, financial weakening, and the closing of factories (or, in the case of a monopoly, into a rise in prices and a reduction of demand)—the world of oligopolies resembles much more closely a race in which, barring any accidents, all reach the finish line, with a greater reward for those who arrive first. It is a sport to which only champions have access, like the Wimbledon Championships.

Thanks to its enormous flexibility, the oligopolistic manner of coordinating decisions was successfully transplanted into the semi-unified space taking shape in the center of the capitalist system. Favoring innovation in all of its forms, the oligopoly constitutes a powerful instrument of economic expansion. Thanks to the freedom of action that oligopolistic firms enjoy, the commerce of manufactured products between core countries has grown with extraordinary speed over the last several decades. On the other hand, the enormous financial capacity these firms tend to accumulate leads them to seek diversification, giving rise to the international conglomerate, which is the most advanced form of modern enterprise.[12]

At first glance, it may seem that the large company derives its strength primarily from economies of scale.[13] This is only partly true. Economies of scale are fundamental in metallurgy, in basic chemistry, in paper production and other industries of continual processes, and also where labor is used in an intensive manner and the work can be organized in a chain. All of this accounts for only one part of modern industry's enormous process of concentration. Its great strength derives from the fact that it works in organized markets—it is able to control prices and, therefore, to guarantee self-financing and plan its long-term activities. But there is no doubt that it was the industries of the first category that constituted the experimental field in which oligopolistic techniques were developed. This is because, where economies of scale are important, the immobilizations of capital are considerable,[14] which facilitates the creation of barriers to entry for new members of the club. Only when these barriers are solid is it possible to control prices and plan for the long term. Furthermore, in this type of industry it is much more difficult to keep plans for expansion hidden. Finally, in the industries that produce homogenous articles, the costs of production are relatively transparent, to the extent to which techniques are known. It is natural, therefore, that companies of this type were the first to organize internationally into oligopolies. And it was the evolution, in core countries, of the industrial input-producing international oligopolistic company that gave rise to one of the first families of diversified companies. Indeed, as large international companies grew in their capacity to control nonferrous metal prices, it became beneficial for them to become significant utilizers of these metals. On the other hand, in order to plan the long-term production of copper it was necessary to be familiar with the evolution of the aluminum economy, for example. Hence the emergence of new forms of oligopoly focused on coordinating the economy—not that of a single product, but of a group of moderately interchangeable products. A clear example of this evolution is that of large petroleum companies: they began to diversify themselves in the field of petrochemistry and in the enormous family of industries it generates, but they also sought to install themselves in competing sectors, from coal to atomic energy.

If we observe these two lines of diversification together, one vertical and the other horizontal, we see that a company that expands in these two directions tends to be led to control economic activities that seem totally disconnected from each other. At some point, the advantages of diversification begin to be of a strictly financial character, since the excess liquidity of one sector can be utilized in another that is occasionally more dynamic. Now, this type of coordination can be attained through financial institutions, which by definition are much more flexible. This evolutionary process therefore tends to lead to financial coordination, through banking and

other similar institutions, and to oligopolistic coordination, on the operational level.[15]

The comments we have made are based on observation of the U.S. economic structure. We have access to
much less information about the forms oligopolies are
assuming in the more heterogenous economic sphere,
which is in the process of coming together in the capitalist
economy's center. What we do know is that the financial
resources put at the disposal of large companies have
grown considerably, that national European banking
systems have undergone a rapid and drastic restruc-
turing process at a regional level, and that the North
American banking system has expanded internationally
at a dizzying rate. We also know that large companies
operate internationally through decision centers that, in
large measure, elude the control of the national governments of their respective countries.[16]

The structural evolution of core countries inevitably
had repercussions in international economic relations.
In this playing field, more than in any other, the large
company had an advantage.[17] In fact, it alone had
the ability to administer resources applied simultaneously in various countries. It was therefore natural for
old international transactions, organized by interme-
diaries who speculated with stocks or played market
shares, to be progressively substituted by transactions
between companies belonging to a group whose activities were coordinated. As these economic activities
were being organized within core countries to permit
more long-term planning of these companies' activities,
there arose the necessity of also planning international
transactions through long-term supply contracts, installation of subsidiaries, or other forms of coordination.

Operating simultaneously in various countries and
executing international transactions among members of

a single group, large companies began to develop sophisticated price management techniques that required great
discipline, at a practical level, within the oligopolies.
The same product could be sold at different prices
in various countries, independent of local production
costs, and the prices used in international transactions
within the same group were fixed, bearing in mind
the diversities of fiscal policies, exchange problems,
etc. These techniques were practiced in the realm of
oligopolies and therefore would not upset markets nor
impede their growth. The particular interest that their
study presents resides in the fact that they permit us
to see the true import of the large company within the
modern capitalist economy.

The most characteristic trait of capitalism in its
current evolutionary phase is the fact that it supersedes the State, whether national or multinational,
with the intent of establishing guiding criteria in the
general interest that will regulate economic activities
as a whole. It is not that States are less worried today
about the collective good. As economies gain greater
stability, the role of the State on the social plane is
amplified. But because both the stability and expansion
of these economies depend fundamentally on international transactions—and because these are under the
control of large companies—the relations of nation-
states with the latter tend to be relations of power.
First, the large company controls innovation within
national economies—the introduction of new processes
and new products—which is certainly the primary
instrument of international expansion. Second, they are
responsible for a large portion of international transactions and effectively restrict initiative to this sphere.
Third, they operate internationally under leadership
that sidesteps, in large measure, the isolated action of

any particular government. Fourth, they maintain great liquidity outside the control of central banks and have easy access to the international financial market.

What we have said in the previous paragraph should not be understood as a decline of political activity, but as a transformation of the functions of States and the emergence of a new form of political organization whose shape is still being defined. Little astuteness is necessary to perceive that, since the Second World War, the capitalist system has operated with a unified political goal, supported by a unified security system. It is to the existence of this relative unity of political leadership that we owe the rapid reconstruction of the economies of Western Europe and of Japan, the process of "decolonization," the organization of the European Single Market, the persistent action of the GATT with the goal of reducing tariffs, the large movements of capital that permitted large companies to acquire international preeminence, and the acceptance of the dollar standard as a substitute for the old gold standard. The difficulty in understanding this process arises because analogical reasoning helps us very little in this case. It is perfectly clear that North American political tutelage was the "natural" result of the last world conflict. That the greatest human and economic sacrifice was borne by the Soviet Union and that the destruction of the military and political power of Germany and Japan benefitted the United States in the capitalist sector are facts of history that we should accept as such. What is worth highlighting is that, once North American political preeminence was established, conditions arose for profound structural modifications to be made in the capitalist system. We cannot affirm that these modifications were desired or in any way planned by the political or economic centers of the United States.

The truth is that from these changes came economic growth that was much more intense, and a rise in standards of living that was much greater in Western Europe and in Japan, relatively speaking. Apparently, North Americans overestimated the relative advantage they had already secured in the economic field, or they overestimated the threats of social subversion and the capacity of the Soviet Union to amplify its sphere of influence. In any case, they organized a security system that encompassed the capitalist world and, in this way, they exercised what was effectively political tutelage over the nation-states that made up this world.

It is possible that North American political tutelage was easily accepted because, on the economic level, it was not connected to a defined project in terms of U.S. interests: it was presented as an instrument for the defense of "Western civilization," which, for practical purposes, was to a large degree confused with the defense of the capitalist system. In this way, a political superstructure was created at a high level, with the primary mission of clearing the ground where the remnants of old nation-states persisted in creating barriers between countries. Structural reconstruction grew out of the international economy. At an internal level, the nation-states amplified their role to reconstruct infrastructures, modernize institutions, intensify capitalization, expand the workforce, etc. All of this contributed, as may be surmised, to strengthen the position of large companies within each country. But it was the action at the international level, promoted by the political superstructure, that opened the door to fundamental transformations, bringing large companies to a position of power *vis-à-vis* nation-states.

The reunification of the center of the capitalist system constitutes, perhaps, the most important consequence of the Second World War. This center appears, today, as a group of about 800 million people. Its political makeup consists of a regime of tutelage, under U.S. control, in which nation-states enjoy considerable autonomy (albeit to different degrees). Nothing seems to inhibit the power superstructure from evolving in one direction or another, whether to further reinforce the North American position, or to admit a degree of participation from other nation-states.[18] It also does not exclude the possibility that a given nation-state may seek to increase its autonomy. The primary problem that arises in this last case is that of relations with large companies. This is most true for the large companies of its own country, which will now be unable to operate with the same flexibility within international oligopolies and will very likely lose ground to their rivals or will shift, partially, to being controlled by a subsidiary located in another country.

The gross product of the capitalist system's center well exceeds 1.5 trillion dollars, as of the beginning of the 1970s. Access to this immense market, characterized by considerable homogeneity in patterns of consumption, constitutes the supreme privilege of large companies. Within this vast market, the so-called international economy constitutes the sector undergoing most rapid expansion, and in which large companies enjoy the most freedom of action. Every attempt to compartmentalize this space on the part of any nation-state, even the United States, will encounter decided resistance from large companies. On the other hand, each attempt to compartmentalize will reduce the rate of accumulation and economic expansion in the system as a whole, and more particularly in the subsystem that takes the initiative to isolate itself. Unless it intends to modify the lifestyle of its population and, in some way, lose in large measure the advantages that result from being part of the center of the capitalist system, any country—regardless of its size—will have to live alongside large companies, run from inside or outside its borders, respecting the autonomy they need to bring together international oligopolies.

Over the course of the last quarter-century, the gross product of the center of the capitalist system has more than tripled, and commercial relations between the national economies that make up this body have grown at an even faster pace. This growth has occurred largely in the sense of greater homogenization, with a relative decline in the United States and an exceptionally intense increase in the per capita income of countries in which it was relatively low, such as Japan and Italy. But, if it is true that growth in the United States has been relatively slow, it is also true that it is large North American companies that have expanded most at the international level. This expansion, in the majority of cases, did not take the form of incremental growth in the commercial transactions of the United States with the countries in which the subsidiaries of its large companies operate. U.S. companies were those who were best prepared to take advantage of the new possibilities created by the structural reforms that occurred in the capitalist system in this period, whether by reason of the greater financial power they enjoyed, or because of the technological advances they had achieved in fundamental fields. But, as the center of the capitalist system evolved toward greater homogenization, the consequences in the North American economy did not take long to manifest themselves. The quicker growth of productivity outside the United States caused a shift in the commercial scales of this country, which began to be invaded by imports from the other industrial nations. Because the dollar was a "reserve" currency, the result was that the United States took on short-term debts on a scale that had until then been inconceivable.[19] This situation yielded two important and different consequences. The first consisted in the formation of a mass of liquidity that facilitated the rapid development of the international financial market, thus expanding the degree of freedom of action for large companies. The second was the recognition that the current international monetary system is based on the dollar and not on gold. The fact that issuing dollars is a privilege of the United States constitutes irrefutable proof that this country exercises exclusive tutelage over the whole of the capitalist system.

It is possible that in the future this tutelage may be shared with other countries, thereby substituting the dollar with a currency whose quantity is regulated by a system of central banks. Having the ability to issue currency of legal international tender, regardless of its own situation of payment balances, is a royal privilege. It is understandable, therefore, that North Americans work not to abandon it. The regime of fixed exchange rates, prolonged for so long, was based on the optimistic hypothesis that the differential of productivity between the United States and other industrialized economies would be maintained. Beyond this hypothesis, it would only be operational in a world in which international economic relations grew slowly, or based themselves on activities in which the comparative advantages would be based on natural phenomena. The abandonment of the convertibility of the dollar into gold and of the fixed nature of exchange rates between primary currencies meant that the dollar was explicitly transformed into the system's center of gravity.

We referred to the fact that subsidiaries of large

North American companies operating in other countries of the capitalist center have grown with greater intensity than their domestic counterparts. Taking advantage of favorable conditions these countries offer and of other even more advantageous conditions they find on the periphery of the capitalist system, these subsidiaries expand rapidly and tend to create asymmetrical relations with the metropole. On the other hand, during the long period of fixed exchange rates, companies in other industrial countries in which productivity grew rapidly—particularly Japan and the Federal Republic of Germany—implanted themselves solidly in the North American market. In this way, a structural situation was created through which imports began to grow more decidedly than exports. Facing this situation with simple exchange measures means periodically raising the prices of essential imports and opening the door to the deterioration of the terms of exchange. In this way, the considerable success of North American companies abroad has its flip side of problems for other sectors of the economy. As the tendencies referred to become more pronounced and prolonged, a point of friction arises between large companies and other sectors of North American society. It is difficult to speculate about the evolution of a process as complex as this one, but we cannot rule out the hypothesis that this will have important consequences in the political structuring of the capitalist world. If the friction grows worse, we may see the appearance of an inclination to more clearly differentiate the system of political tutelage over the capitalist world from interests more specific to the U.S. nation-state. The current polarized political crisis that is Watergate, through which the legislative power seeks to recuperate some of the constitutional powers that were appropriated by the executive branch over the course of recent years, may be the prelude to important readjustments at a political-institutional level. Reinforcing the legislative power will very likely bring with it greater mobilization of the interests that conflict with large companies, while at the same time making it possible to reduce the capacity of the United States government to exercise international tutelage. Under this hypothesis, it is perfectly possible that the tutelage system will be restructured on more "international" bases.

3
Large Companies in New Center–Periphery Relations

The structural modifications happening in the center, to which we have referred, should be taken into account in any attempt to identify the current evolutionary tendencies of the capitalist system as a whole. First, it is necessary to understand that the process of unification gave way to a considerable acceleration of growth in the center. Indeed, the average growth rate in the bloc of countries that form the center has more than doubled over the course of the last quarter-century, with respect to the historical growth rate of these same countries. Second, the divide that already separated the system's center from its periphery has widened considerably, which in large measure is simply the result of the acceleration of growth in the center. Third, commercial relations between core and peripheral countries, even more than those among core countries, have progressively transformed into the internal operations of large companies.

Having never known the phase in which a relatively autonomous national economic system was formed—a phase that allowed for the integration of internal structures and the homogenization of technology—peripheral economies undergo a process in which internal disparities become increasingly aggravated as they become more industrialized, led by import substitution. We have referred to this fact before—an inevitable consequence of a poor country's attempts to reproduce the lifestyles of countries that have already attained much higher levels of capital accumulation. Now, this type of industrialization—which in earlier periods was impeded by considerable obstacles arising from the lack of capital, the difficulty in accessing technology, the small size of the internal market—is now being carried out with extraordinary speed, thanks to the cooperation of international oligopolies.[1] By using financed technology (along with equipment that at times is also financed) and mobilizing local capital, large companies have the means to install industries in the majority of peripheral countries, particularly if these industries are partially integrated with importation activities.

Needless to say, the industrialization that is currently taking place in the periphery under the control of large companies is a qualitatively distinct process from the industrialization that, in a previous phase, core countries underwent and—further still—from the kind they experience today. The economic dynamism[2] in the center of the system results from the flow of new products and the raising of real wages, which permits the expansion of mass consumption. In contrast, peripheral capitalism engenders cultural mimicking and requires permanent concentration of income in order for minorities to reproduce the consumption patterns of core countries. This point is essential for coming to grips with the global structure of the capitalist system. While in core capitalism the accumulation of capital has expanded over the course of the last century with undeniable stability in income distribution (both functionally and socially), in peripheral capitalism industrialization continues to exacerbate growing income concentration.[3]

Over the last quarter-century, the evolution of the capitalist system has been characterized by a process of homogenization and integration of the center, a growing distance between the center and the periphery, and a considerable widening of the divide that, inside the periphery, separates a privileged minority from the large masses of the population. These processes are not independent of one another; they should be considered as part of the same evolutionary framework. The integration of the center has allowed its economic growth rate to intensify, which is responsible in large measure for widening the divide that separates it from the periphery. On the other hand, the intensity of growth in the center conditions the orientation of industrialization in the periphery, since the privileged minorities of this group seek to reproduce the lifestyle of the center. In other words, the more intense the flow of new products in the center becomes (which is increasingly a function of average income), the quicker the concentration of revenue will occur in the periphery.

The intensification of growth in the center results from the confluence of various factors, one of the most important of which is the economies of scale permitted by the growing homogenization and unification of what used to be national markets. Because industrialization (which occurs concurrently in the periphery) relies on import substitution, at the level of small markets, it is natural that the productivity gap would tend to rise and structural discontinuity within the capitalist system would grow. It is important to note that, in the context of capitalism, large companies' growing control over economic activity in the center and the way technological progress leans toward mass production increasingly hinder the long-overdue creation of national economic systems. Of course, the situation varies in the periphery from one country to another, based on population, availability of natural resources, revenue levels previously attained, dynamism of traditional exports, capacity for taking on external debt, etc. In countries with large populations, the simple concentration of income can allow for the formation of a market that is sufficiently large and diversified.

What can be said of the evolutionary tendencies of relations between the center and the periphery from the structural framework we have just outlined? We referred to the fact that one of the characteristics of this framework is the growing internalization, within large companies, of commercial transactions between countries.[4] We also observed that, as they emerged, many of the industrial activities on the periphery were integrated with import flows. In this way, a single company controls industrial units in a core country (or in more than one), those in various peripheral countries, and the commercial transactions between these distinct productive units. The situation is similar to that of a company that integrates itself vertically within a country: it operates a coal mine, a steel mill, a pipe factory, etc. There is, however, an important difference arising from the fact that in the first case the distinct productive units are inserted in various monetary systems. This creates the problem of exchanging one currency with another, which requires finding another company that will carry out an equivalent operation in reverse, or carrying out this operation inside the same company (or in another of the same group). Traditionally, these clearing operations are done by banks. Given the unpredictable exchange and monetary situations of many peripheral countries, however, a large company that operates internationally may prefer to create its own structure of exchanges, establishing an internal system of prices that allows it to plan its activities on a longer-term basis.

Let us examine a case that is not typical but that reveals the root of the problem. Imagine a petroleum company operating in the Venezuela that existed before its current fiscal complications. This company produced a certain amount of petroleum for the internal market, the prices of which could be more or less manipulated in such a way as to allow the company to obtain the necessary amount of local currency to cover all of its local expenditures. Part of what was produced would be exported to pay for its imported inputs, including capital depreciation. The rest of what was produced (the majority, by far) would be exported and would represent the liquid revenue from the invested capital. In this extreme situation, the company can ignore the existence of exchange rates; if costs in the local currency rise, the price of locally sold petroleum also rises.

Let us consider now the more regular case of a sewing machine factory whose products are sold entirely in the internal market. The sales revenue, after covering local expenses, is taken to the Central Bank to be exchanged into foreign currencies, in order to pay for the imported inputs and to replenish the capital. If the Central Bank creates difficulties in the distribution of dividends, the company may be tempted to arbitrarily raise the costs of imported inputs: special materials, patents, technical assistance, etc.

Suppose that cases like this multiply, and that companies in this situation arise on every side.[5] This would increase the pressure on the balance of payments and would relentlessly depreciate the exchange rate in such a marked way that internal price levels could not be raised to keep up. Because capital is accounted for in dollars, profitability could only be maintained if the company's sales prices grew in like measure, which would tend to stall industrial activity. Alternatively, let us imagine another scenario for our sewing machine factory. Let us suppose that the manufacturer generates sufficient revenue in the internal market to cover its costs in local currency, including taxes and local financial expenditures; that afterwards it exports pieces of machines to its headquarters or to other subsidiaries, as a way of compensating for the inputs that it imports; and that, with the remaining productive capacity, it develops a production line for the international market, earning revenue in the form of foreign currencies to replenish the capital. In this way, the company can practically isolate itself from the exchange system of the subsidiary's country. Because the company is interested in growing, it will have to adopt a pricing policy for both the internal and external markets capable of promoting the sale of the product. However, at each level of production it will have to distribute its productive capacity between the two markets, keeping in mind that, after a certain point, exchange rate fees will be applied to the revenue obtained in local currency.

Suppose the company limits its sales in the internal market to what is necessary to cover its expenses in local currency and that it compensates the importation of inputs by selling pieces directly to headquarters. In this case, the gross profit corresponds to the sales in the international market. Comparing this profit to the capital invested in the subsidiary, the company reaches its rate of profit without going through the monetary system of the subsidiary's country. If the same company undertakes operations of this nature with various subsidiaries, it is natural for it to ask which factors are responsible for the differences in profitability between them. If we presume the technology to be about the same, the primary factors causing the difference in profitability will be as follows: scale of production, local external economies, cost of inputs that cannot be imported, and cost of local taxes in terms of the final product. The first three factors are directly linked to the size of the internal market. In this way, if we assume that the level of taxes is the same, the relative profitability becomes dependent on the relative size of the internal market and on the cost of labor in terms of final production. Now, the positive effect of the size of the local market moves toward a point of saturation, which varies from industry to industry. As this saturation point for a given industry is reached, the fundamental factor shifts to being the cost of labor for the final product sold on the international market.[6]

If we view the panorama we have created from another angle, we see that as the large company organizes a productive system that extends from center to periphery, it is effectively able to incorporate into the center's economy the resources of cheap labor from the periphery. Indeed, a large company that orients its investments toward the periphery is capable of increasing its competitive capacity, thanks to the utilization of cheaper labor for the products it launches on the market. The situation is similar to that of companies that use temporary immigrants, paying them wages that are much lower than those which prevail in their own country. Let us imagine that an American company located on the border with Mexico (but on the United States side) utilizes Mexican labor, paid in Mexican currency, according to wage levels in Mexico. Crossing the border daily, these workers would continue to reside in their own country and spend money in Mexico. Let us further imagine that this country exports products to Mexico priced to exactly match the expenses incurred in Mexican pesos. The social legislation that prevails today in practically the entire world inhibits this type of "exploitation" of laborers, but it is considered normal that the same American factory can locate itself on the Mexican side of the border, use local labor and pay them local wages, and then sell its products in the United States. An intermediary formula that is increasingly used consists of attracting temporary immigrants and paying them higher wages than those that prevail in their countries of origin, but lower than those that would be paid to laborers coming from the core country. In various countries of Western Europe, foreign labor— considered "temporary"—accounts for roughly 10% of the workforce. In the case of Switzerland, it represents one-third of the non-specialized workforce.

There is no estimate about the volume of cheap labor used directly in peripheral countries by large companies in manufacturing production destined for the international market. But, because of the rising costs of temporary immigrant labor, under pressure from local unions and from social problems that arise when the mass of socially disenfranchised workers grows beyond certain limits, we can expect large companies' preferred solution to be the utilization of labor directly in the periphery. On the other hand, this solution tends to reinforce the position of these companies *vis-à-vis* nation-states. In summary: a situation is emerging that permits the large company to use technology and capital from the center and labor (and capital) from the periphery, considerably increasing its power to maneuver. This reinforces the aforementioned tendency toward the "internationalization" of economic activities within the capitalist system.

We said before that, over the last quarter-century, international economic activities are those that have grown most quickly in the center of the capitalist system. Now, the relations that are being established between the center and the periphery at the level of large companies have begun to give rise to a new type of international activity that may come to constitute the segment that is most rapidly expanding in the system as a whole. We are left to question whether it is appropriate to continue calling these activities "international." When the economist thinks in terms of international commerce, he has in mind transactions between economic units that are integrated in distinct national economies. The problem is less one of immobility of factors (as the formulations of the first economists who theorized about this matter lead us to believe) than of the existence of relatively autonomous systems of costs and prices. In other words, from the moment in which we posit the existence of a national economic system inside which productive resources possess an "opportunity cost" based on the better uses that could be made of them, the option between producing good A for the internal market or producing another good for the external market (and importing good A) should have an optimal solution. It is clear that, if multiple options are being discussed, extending through diverse time periods, with retroactive repercussions of one upon each other, the problem will never be adequately considered, much less solved. But this is different than saying that the theory is "wrong."

Now, from the moment the category of "national economic system" cannot be taken into account, the theorem cannot be formulated. Let us return to the example of the sewing machine factory that is installed in a peripheral country and that replenishes its capital with part of the very production it exports. In this case, there is no counterpart of imports, but this does not invalidate the theory of comparative advantages. The imports, in this case, are substituted by the flow of capital and technology that marks the presence, in the country, of a large company managed from abroad. All of this happens as if the peripheral country, which has at its disposal a stock of labor, were forced to choose between: a) using part of this labor force to produce good X destined for the external market, and being able in this way to pay for the imported sewing machines; or b) using part of this labor force to replenish capital and foreign technology installed in the country and—in combination with another contingent of laborers—to produce these same sewing machines for the internal market. This rationale would be correct if the reference point from which decisions are made were constituted by the national economic system—in other words, if the congruence of the decisions were internally established, figuring in the price of external resources as a simple parameter of the problem. However, reality seems to be totally different. Decisions are made by the large company, for which the cost of labor in a peripheral country, in terms of an article it produces in that country and commercializes abroad, is simply a number.

The large company that exports capital and technology from the United States to Mexico, and installs a factory there whose production is destined for the North American market—there being considerable unemployment in the United States (the social cost of labor is zero)—makes decisions based on a reference point that supersedes the North American market considered in its strict sense. The large company that diverts financial resources from one peripheral country (because wages in that country begin to rise) in order to invest them in another where labor is cheaper, is also making decisions based on a wider context. The problem is not limited, however, to the narrow realm of options for using the scarce resources we conceive of abstractly. The truth is that the large company has as its foremost directive to expand, and to this end it tends to occupy positions in the various areas of the capitalist system.[7] The countries from the center of the system constitute the most important areas by far, which is the reason why technological efforts are primarily geared toward functioning in these countries. Production plans in peripheral countries are conditioned by this same technological orientation, and the internal markets of these countries are molded to the convenience of the global action of this company.

It would be a mistake to conclude from the observations above that large companies act outside any kind of reference point, which would imply denying, if not rationality, then at least efficiency in its behavior. But it seems beyond question that this behavior, very frequently, transcends whatever kind of reference point corresponds to a national economic system. What is more, in peripheral countries the growing activity of these companies tends to create economic structures that are difficult to think of from the perspective of a "national economic system." The reference point of large companies tends increasingly to be the whole of the capitalist system, a reference that encompasses an economic universe that is very heterogeneous, and whose biggest discontinuity derives from the gulf that exists between center and periphery. In this world of great complexity, full of national borders, with an immense variety of monetary and fiscal systems, and teeming with local political quarrels that occasionally drag on in the form of wars—all of this under a weak and decentralized tutelage—large companies cannot aspire to do more than arrive at mediocre situations. Notwithstanding the immense resources they dedicate to obtaining information and the sophisticated means they use to interpret that information, construct models, simulate scenarios, etc., in practice they must content themselves with simple rules. Indeed, the exceptional success of some is attributed by analysts of the profession to the intuition of "extraordinary men," thus repeating an old legend of political history.

The idea espoused by some scholars of the current evolution of capitalism that core economies lean toward growing integration at a national level—in the face of the *indicative* flattening, or of the cartelization and interpenetration of large groups with organs of the State—has an element of truth but leaves out the essence of the evolution of capitalism over the last quarter-century. It is beyond question that, for the last three decades, industrialized capitalist economies have been operating with a degree of internal coordination far superior to what had until then been considered compatible with a market economy. This coordination, inspired by Keynes, essentially constitutes a social victory. Thanks to it, the human and social costs of the operation of capitalist economies have been considerably reduced. It is also probable that this greater coordination has had positive repercussions in medium- and long-term growth rates. But this is just a hypothesis. Little doubt exists, however, that the increase in growth rates is connected to economies of scale, to intense technological exchange, and to movement of capital, which have accompanied the process of integration of core economies. Without the simultaneous effort of greater internal coordination at a national level, the international expansion under the aegis of large companies would (most likely) have caused local breakdowns, greater geographic concentration of economic activity, and—possibly—reactions in the political sphere that may have impeded the process of core integration. It is known, for example, that the strong dynamism of the external sector gives rise to internal tensions that would be particularly serious if these economies had not developed such sophisticated techniques of internal coordination. In this way, it is also possible to affirm that this advance in internal coordination accelerated integration on an international level. In summary, the action of nation-states in the center of the system was amplified in specific directions to assure internal stability, without which international friction would be inevitable. On the other hand, however, it was qualitatively modified in order to adapt to the operation of large companies structured within oligopolies, which have the initiative at the technological level and are the true driving force at an international level.

The complex relations that exist between the governments of core countries, whether isolated or in subgroups (the "ten richest," the European Economic Community, etc.), between these governments and large companies (which, in specific cases, act in coordination), between them and international institutions (which are almost always under the control of the U.S. government), and finally, between them and the government of the United States itself, whose hegemonic position in particular points is often contested—all this network of relations cannot easily be perceived with clarity. This is not just because there is a lack of monographic studies about many of its fundamental aspects, but primarily because this network is in a process of structuring. Experience has shown that the margin of flexibility that States possess to act in the economic sphere is relatively narrow. If an economy undergoes a shift, external pressures for its respective government to adopt certain measures can be considerable. These pressures are exerted by other governments, by international institutions, and by large companies directly. It is also fitting to note that these last have a mass of liquid resources at their disposal that is far superior to the reserves of the network of central banks. The situation of the government of the United States is certainly special, among many reasons, because it issues the currency that constitutes the base of the international monetary system. However, the experience of 1972 made it clear that the government of this country cannot launch itself into a policy of "full employment" while neglecting the repercussions in the balance of payments. If external short-term debt surpasses a certain critical quota, large companies can exert sufficient pressure on the dollar to force the U.S. government to choose between devaluing the currency or changing the trajectory of internal policies.[8]

Any speculation about the evolution, in coming years, of the network of relations that makes up the new superstructure of the capitalist system (currently in the process of unification) has a strictly exploratory value. Two general tendencies seem to take shape: on the one hand, the process of integration tends to strengthen large companies; on the other hand, the necessity of ensuring stability in the internal sphere of each national subsystem requires growing efficiency and sophistication in the operation of the States. The current situation is one of alliance between large companies and the respective governments to obtain internal and external advantages. But we also observe joint efforts of companies from various countries, attempting to exert pressure on governments—including their own. Experience has shown that government control of a large company's capital does not necessarily affect its behavior in this regard in a substantial way. Companies, no matter how large they may be, are relatively simple organizations in terms of their objectives. Being highly bureaucratized, they possess a large degree of internal coherency, which facilitates and requires clear objectives. The State, in a society of classes in which rival groups compete and almost always share power in some way, constitutes a much more complex institution, with objectives that are less defined and ever changing, and therefore less linear in their evolution. There is no doubt that large companies enjoy considerable power in the social sphere, because they control the most powerful forms of invention, those founded on technology and on control of production equipment. But when society, or segments of society, reacts to the asphyxiation created by the use of this power, the waves that arise have repercussions in State structures, from which corrective measures occasionally issue. We can grant the hypothesis that it is precisely the international expansion of large companies that favors the liberation of the State from the tutelage they exercise today in their respective countries. In other words: as the large company supports itself internationally to expand its power, it may encounter more difficulty in assuming command, in taking on the mantle of the "national interest" inside its own country. There would be a provincialization of States, but a more effectual representativity of the distinct segments of civil society would lend itself to the political power to exercise the increasingly necessary guiding role of social life. If the evolution occurs in this direction, we must admit that tensions will arise between nation-states and large companies, or groups of large companies—tensions that will become an important factor in transformations of the system in its entirety. They may become aggravated and open gaps capable of bringing about qualitative, reorienting changes in all parts of the evolutionary process, but they may also provoke reactions at the level of the tutelary superstructure. This would lead to a greater institutionalization of this structure and to the constitution of organs bestowed with coercive power, whose objective would be to preserve the integrity of the system.[9]

The comments in the previous paragraph are simple conjectures suggested by the observation of certain tendencies of the capitalist system's structural evolution. They do not intend to mean that class struggles will be attenuated, and much less that this State—semi-provincialized, but nonetheless a State responsible for the stability of a society of classes—will be the simple administrator of a consensus that will permeate all social life. It is possible that the working classes will come to have growing clout in the orientation of a State that should come to an understanding with the system of large companies based on positions of strength. Under this hypothesis, it follows that the evolution of the working classes would be geared toward growing identification with the national societies to which they belong, or rather, with a project of social development that can be monitored from the decision-making centers that participate in the State. This does not necessarily mean that they tend toward a kind of *nationalism*, but rather that their concerns would tend to focus on the plane of political action, upon which they will have increasing influence. In a parallel manner, the growing clout of the directing groups of large companies in the capitalist class cannot avoid influencing the vision this class has of the world, of the *dépassement* of the national panorama. To feel part of an "international class," which today is characteristic of the upper levels of the bureaucracy of these companies, would tend to be a generalized attitude of the upper layers of the capitalist class. The distance between the ideological attitude of these layers and the class of small capitalists not yet caught in the net of large companies' subcontractors would tend to increase. The small local company, presented earlier as an anachronism with high social cost, comes to be defended as part of a threatened cultural landscape. Between *poujadisme* and the defense of quality of life there is an important evolution with repercussions in the power relations between social classes.

The role of the tutelary superstructure of the capitalist system is not limited to promoting the ideology of integration and to occasionally arbitrating regional conflicts. This superstructure has a history, which is essentially linked to the delimitation of the system's borders. We can admit, at the level of conjecture, that core capitalist economies would always move, in one phase of their history, toward a process of integration. But there is no doubt that the speed with which this integration has advanced in the last quarter-century, and the shape it has taken, are directly linked to the existence of a group of noncapitalist countries, considered by the directing groups to represent external and internal threats to the capitalist system. The quick and enthusiastic acceptance of U.S. leadership by the directing capitalist groups in Germany and Japan would be difficult to explain without the psychological climate created by the Cold War. Psychological mobilization was essential for border demarcation, but its consolidation required negotiating with the adversary about a set of rules of behavior. The tutelary superstructure has the roles of ensuring border integrity and of coming to an understanding with the adversary at any moment in which unsolved or new problems threaten to extend beyond their mutual control. As a basic system of communication was agreed upon, and as the fundamental interests of the two blocs were mutually recognized, possibilities for mutually advantageous economic relations were created. That these possibilities were quickly exploited by large companies constitutes a clear indication of the extraordinary capacity of these organizations to operate at an international level. This is a fact of considerable importance, because it reveals the capacity large companies have to adapt to distinct forms of social organization. It is a simple indication of practicality, since the behavior of large companies is anything but ideologically neutral. The recent action of the ITT company in Chile is there to show that many of them are not reluctant, in a confrontation in which the ideological element is present, to practice acts of true international banditry.[10] However, other experiences, such as that of Guinea, reveal that they are also preparing to defend their interests without giving too much attention to local ideological quarrels. It seems clear that a social mutation in an important country of the capitalist system's center—which would imply a loss of large companies' control of technology and of the orientation of the forms of consumption—could not happen without provoking a large reaction. But everything leads us to believe that large companies, faced with a situation that is difficult to reverse, would adapt, since in a bureaucracy the survival instinct always tends to prevail, even though this might occasionally require important removals of those in power.

4

Options for Peripheral Countries

The new forms capitalism is taking in peripheral countries are not independent from the global evolution of the system. It seems undeniable, however, that the periphery will have growing importance in this evolution, not only because core countries will be increasingly dependent on nonrenewable natural resources supplied by it, but also because large companies will find in the exploitation of its cheap labor one of the principal points of support to solidify themselves in the system more broadly. But if it is difficult to speculate about tendencies with respect to the center, it is even more so when they relate to the periphery, whose social structures and institutional composition have been studied little, or have been seen under the distorted light of analogies with other historical processes.

The most important fact to highlight, as it relates to the peripheral countries in a more advanced process of industrialization, is the considerable difficulty in coordinating their economies at an internal level, because of the way they are interacting with the international economy in the context of large companies. If difficulties in internal coordination exist in core countries, as we have seen, the problem gains even more complexity in the periphery. I do not refer to the classic situation of the small country where the level of public spending and the situation of the balance of payments reflect decisions made by a large company that exports natural resources. The situation is distinct, but no more comfortable in those countries in which the primary industrial activities linked to the internal market are controlled by large companies with their own projects of international expansion, of which little knowledge is held by the governments of the countries in which they operate. This weakness of the State, as an instrument of direction and coordination of economic activities, on behalf of something that can be defined as the interest of the local collectivity, becomes a significant factor in the evolutionary process. Despite its impotence in fundamental things, the State has great responsibilities in the construction and operation of basic services, in the guarantee of legal order, in the imposition of discipline over the working masses. The growth of the State apparatus is inevitable, and the necessity of perfecting its higher levels becomes a demand of the large companies that invest in the country.

In this way, the growing insertion of peripheral economies into the international playing field of large companies is contributing to the modernization of State bureaucracies, which have begun to gain considerable autonomy. Being on the one hand impotent and on the other necessary and efficient, these bureaucracies tend to multiply initiatives in various directions. The orientation of economic activities, imposing the concentration of profits and bringing about the coexistence of lavish consumer spending with the misery of the great masses, is the origin of social tensions that inevitably have repercussions at the political level. The State, incapable of modifying the orientation mentioned, exhausts itself in the fight against its effects. Political frustrations lead to institutional instability and to control of the State by the armed forces, which contributes to reinforcing its bureaucratic character even more. In summary, the growing "international" control of the economic activities of peripheral countries leads to premature autonomy on the part of the State bureaucratic apparatus. This apparatus is frequently controlled from outside the country, but, on every side, it is subject to being spurred on by groups coming from the local political process. Nevertheless, what prevails is a feeling of powerlessness, which results from fundamental economic activities finding themselves dependent on foreign decision-making centers.

The relative autonomy of the bureaucracies that control States on the periphery reflects, to a certain degree, the modifications that have occurred in the political superstructure of the capitalist system as a whole. The destruction of traditional forms of colonialism should be understood as part of the process of destruction of institutional barriers that compartmentalized the capitalist world. As the international economy began to be controlled by large companies, the direct involvement of core States in the administration of peripheral countries became unnecessary, being commonly denounced as discriminatory and as favoring companies of a certain nationality.[1] It is known that this process happened in an irregular manner: in some cases, "expatriate" populations constituted a strong source of pressure, demanding the direct or indirect presence of the old metropole, which gives rise to other, masked forms of colonialism. At other times directing groups, threatened with losing control over the local power system, appeal for external political support. But overall, direct intervention in peripheral countries by the governments of core countries has generally been exceptional, if we set aside U.S. interventions linked to the "defense" of the system's borders.

Within this structural framework, the bureaucracies that direct the majority of peripheral countries advanced considerably in a process of self-identification with their respective "national interests." Although, in particular cases, these interests are confused with those of the small group that controls the State apparatus, as a rule the conception of national interest is wider and focuses on improving the living conditions of an important part of the population, almost always constituted by those who are integrated into the "modern" sector of the economy.

One of the sectors in which peripheral States have exercised their autonomy, in the face of large companies, is in the control of nonrenewable natural resources from their respective countries. The expansion of the system in the center depends increasingly on access to the source of these resources, located in the periphery. We referred to the situation of the United States, which is, from this point of view, a privileged country. Demand for natural resources does not grow in parallel with per capita income; after reaching a certain income level, it tends to stabilize. For example, the consumption of copper per inhabitant tripled in the United States between 1900 and 1940, but it remained stable between then and 1970; the consumption of steel per inhabitant in this same country grew more than three times between 1900 and 1950, but it remained stable between then and 1970.[2] On the other hand, the consumption of metals by the industry can be higher or lower, independent of the income level, by virtue of the nature of the country's exports. However, if we take into account that the average income level of the population group at the center of the system (not counting the United States) is less than half that of this country, it becomes clear that the demand for metals will continue to grow in the center for many years to come, in a way that is much more intense than the growth of the population. If we add to this that the most easily accessed reserves in core countries are running out, it is easy to understand the growing "dependence" of these countries *vis-à-vis* nonrenewable resources from the periphery. This dependence will continue to grow even if consumption of the resources discussed stabilizes in the center, which is in no way probable in the foreseeable future.

The use of reserves of natural resources as an instrument of power by peripheral States requires articulation between countries that is by no means an easy task. But that this articulation is already happening, with apparent success in the case of petroleum, represents an indication of the considerable sophistication being achieved by the bureaucracies that control these States.[3] It is true that large companies will not always be hostile to this policy, since, as it involves a product with inelastic demand, the rise of prices cannot avoid having favorable repercussions on its rates, since it almost always means a rise in profits. Clearly, the situation will be different if peripheral countries aim for total control over the production and commercialization of these products. Even so, the advantage these large companies have, as it relates to their organizational capacity and technology, assures them the possibility of continuing to negotiate in a position of power for a long time.

It so happens, however, that the most important nonrenewable resources, whose prices can be effectively controlled by peripheral countries—assuming they succeed in positioning themselves effectively—are very unequally distributed. The recent case of petroleum brought to light the considerable transfers of resources that can happen inside the periphery itself as a result of this type of policy. The real benefits for certain countries are important, but these countries house a small minority of the population that lives in the periphery. A large part of the new financial resources they have at their disposal will necessarily have to be invested in the center of the system. What happens, then, is a transfer of assets that will transform part of the population of the beneficiary countries into rentiers, without the structure of the capitalist economy being modified in a significant manner. It is also possible that the beneficiary countries put part of the resources referred to at the disposal of other peripheral countries. But, if such resources are used to reinforce the development process as it is now—for example, to create infrastructure and basic industries that generate external economies for large companies—the relations between the center and the periphery will not change in any appreciable way.

The policy of raising relative prices of products that are not easily substitutable, and which peripheral countries export, surely represents a milestone in the evolution of these countries. But, as we have indicated, it does not mean a course change in the evolutionary process of the capitalist system as a whole. It does not eliminate the hypothesis that the international position of large companies may be strengthened, as they undertake to absorb a large portion of the new liquid resources directed toward the international financial market. A small part of the peripheral population, located in a few countries, will have access to the most advanced forms of consumption, and a few States will be able to rise to assume a hegemonic role in certain limited areas. However, modifications in the periphery as a whole will hardly be perceptible.

But it is possible that the experience gained in the sector of nonrenewable resources may come to be utilized in defense of the real value of labor, which large companies exploit in peripheral countries. As has been mentioned before, the rapid expansion of the international economy—the most dynamic sector of the capitalist system—tends to be based on the utilization of large reserves of cheap labor that exist in the periphery. Two problems arise here: that of appropriating the fruits of economic expansion and that of the general orientation of the process of accumulation. Given the large disparity between the lifestyles we currently see on the periphery, large companies are in a position of strength to keep wages at the lowest levels. Any pressure to raise them can be contained by diverting investments to other areas that offer more favorable conditions.[4] The large company that produces manufactured products on the periphery for the center market has a margin of maneuver that gets larger the lower the wages being paid. This margin allows it to expand the market in the short term or to increase its capacity for self-financing. In either case, the higher the margin, the higher the portion of value added that remains outside the peripheral country in which the industry is located.

Everything happens as if labor were a resource to be exported, with wage rates being the cost of exporting. If the aggregate of peripheral countries decided to double the price of exporting its workforce in terms of international currency, the result would be similar to what happens when prices rise for an export product that enjoys inelastic demand in the center. In reality, this rise in price has taken place in special situations.

For example, years ago workers in the copper industry in Chile were able to secure a considerable increase in their wages with respect to the "offer price" of their labor. This raise could have been taken further, but the Chilean government preferred to use the direct taxation method to widen the margin of value added by this industry that was retained in the country. When talking about a manufacturing industry with multiple production lines whose export prices can be easily manipulated, it is more difficult to use the fiscal route. Indeed, how can we determine the profitability of the partner of a large company installed in a country in southeast Asia, if the prices of all of the inputs used are controlled by its headquarters, along with the prices of the exported products?

It is difficult to conjecture about a general increase of real wages in the export activities of peripheral countries. Because wage rates vary greatly among peripheral countries, the consequences would be different from one country to the next, particularly if the increase were done to achieve greater equalization. We must remember that, depending on each country's general level of development, the workforce's use of a similar technology can result in varying levels of physical productivity. The equalization of wage rates, in the industrial export activities of peripheral countries, would therefore tend to benefit those that are (relatively) more industrially advanced. The problem is certainly much more complex than raising the price of a homogenous product that enjoys inelastic demand in the center. But it is along this route that, sooner or later, peripheral countries will have to advance to take control of a larger portion of the fruits of their own workforce. If large companies continue to pay wages that correspond to the "offer price" of the labor force in the periphery, the very process of industrialization of peripheral countries will contribute to widen the gap that separates them from the center of the system.

The policy of increasing real wage rates we referred to in previous paragraphs would have as a direct consequence the creation of a wage differential[5] between the sector linked to exportation and the rest of the local economy. This would result in the formation of a new social layer, semi-integrated into "modern" forms of consumption. Because the degree of accumulation reached in the economy does not allow this wage rate to be generalized, the root of the problem of underdevelopment would not change. To reach this root, it would be necessary for the resources retained in the peripheral country to be used in a cumulative process, aimed at modifying the structure of the economic system toward a growing homogenization. The ultimate question is in the orientation of the accumulation process, and this orientation would remain in the hands of large companies. It is important to note that adopting this orientation—establishing priorities on behalf of coherent social objectives compatible with the push for accumulation—would be the only way to free the economy from the tutelage of large companies. This path is not easy, and it is natural for the bureaucracies that control peripheral States to feel little attraction to it. However, the growing social tensions that generate the system's current structural tendencies can force many of these bureaucracies to follow unforeseen paths. This includes the path of a genuine concern for social interests and that of searching for ways to coexist with large companies that are compatible with internal orientation of the development process.

5

The Myth of Economic Development

If we set aside conjectures and limit ourselves to observing the structural setup present in the capitalist system, we see that the process of accumulation tends to widen the gap between an increasingly homogenized center and a constellation of peripheral economies whose disparities continue to intensify. In truth, large companies' growing hegemony in orienting the process of accumulation translates, in the center, into a tendency toward the homogenization of consumption patterns and, in peripheral economies, into a distancing of a privileged minority's ways of life from those of the masses. This orientation of the accumulation process is, in itself, sufficient for the pressure on nonrenewable resources to be substantially lower than that which is the basis for the alarmist projections mentioned earlier.

It is necessary to distinguish between two types of resource pressure. The first is linked to the idea of the Malthusian trap: it refers to the availability of arable land to be used in the context of subsistence agriculture. In countries in which a large part of the population lives close to the subsistence level, the availability of arable lands (or the possibility of intensifying their cultivation through small increases in the costs of production in terms of unskilled labor) is a decisive factor in determining the demographic growth rate. There is no doubt that access to land can be impeded by institutional factors and that local food supply can be reduced by the expansion of export cultures. In both cases, pressure on resources increases if there is a dense rural population that depends on subsistence agriculture. The effects of this type of resource pressure only multiply when the population has the option to emigrate; generally speaking, they dissipate within the borders of each country. What is important to highlight is that this type of resource pressure can precipitate calamities in specific areas, such as those currently occurring in Africa's Sahel region, but it has minimal effect on the functioning of the system as a whole.

The second type of pressure on resources is caused by direct and indirect effects of increases in populations' level of consumption; it is directly linked to the general orientation of the process of development. The fact that income continues to be considerably concentrated in countries with higher standards of living aggravates the resource pressure that the process of economic growth naturally generates. We can also affirm that the growing income concentration in the center of the system—that is, the widening of the gap that separates the periphery from this center—constitutes an additional factor in the increase of pressure on nonrenewable resources. In fact, if it were better distributed across the capitalist system as a whole, growth would depend less on the introduction of new finished products and more on widespread use of more familiar products, which would mean a lower waste coefficient. Capitalization tends to be more intense the more growth is oriented toward the introduction of new finished products—that is, toward the shortening of the useful life of goods already incorporated into the patrimony of people and the collective. In this way, the simple geographic concentration of income, for the benefit of countries that enjoy a higher level of consumption, generates greater pressure on nonrenewable resources.

If the first type of resource pressure is localized and checks itself, the second is cumulative and exerts pressure on the system as a whole. The alarmist projections of the study *The Limits to Growth* refer, in their essence, to this second type of pressure. Relationships between capital accumulation and pressure on resources, which are the basis of these projections, are founded on empirical observations and can be accepted as a valid initial approximation. What cannot be accepted is the hypothesis, also implicit in these projections, according to which the current consumption patterns of rich countries move toward being generalized on a planetary scale. This hypothesis directly contradicts the general orientation of development that is currently underway in the system as a whole, which results in the exclusion of large masses living in peripheral countries from the benefits this development creates. Indeed, it is precisely those who are excluded that make up the demographic mass in rapid expansion.

In the 1970s, the population of the capitalist world is currently made up of approximately 2.5 billion individuals. Of this total, about 800 million live in the system's center, and 1.7 billion on its periphery. The evolutionary tendency of these two population groups is defined in their fundamental trajectories, and there is no evidence that it will change over the course of the next few decades as a consequence of one or another type of pressure on the resources we discussed. This being the case (and if we exclude the hypothesis of a substantial migratory flux from the periphery to the center), it follows that the population of core countries as a whole will reach 1.2 billion inhabitants within the next century. Most scholars of this topic accept the belief that this demographic mass will move toward stabilizing over the next few decades. The situation presented by the second demographic subgroup is much more complex in its dynamics. In this case, the pressure on the first type of resources performs a fundamental role. However, if we take into account the age structure of this population, of which roughly half currently finds itself under the age of procreation, it seems beyond doubt that birth rates will remain high for a few generations. This is one of the consequences of the orientation of development that—by concentrating income for the benefit of rich countries and rich minorities in poor countries—reduces the effect of the increase in income levels on birth rates, with respect to the system as a whole. It is likely that, over the course of the 21st century, the population of the periphery will double every 33 years, which means that it will grow from 1.7 billion to 13.6 billion. This being the case, the population of core countries would multiply by 1.5, and that of peripheral countries by 8, resulting in the population as a whole going from 2.5 billion to 14.8 billion. In other words, it would multiply by 5.9.

With respect to pressure on the second type of resources—that is, the cumulative pressure capable of generating tensions in the system as a whole—the center-periphery division is less significant than the division between those who benefit from the process of capital accumulation and those whose living conditions are only marginally or indirectly affected by this process. In other words, the gap that the current orientation of development is creating within peripheral countries is more important than the other gap existing between them and the system's center. Information about income distribution in peripheral countries makes it clear that the segment of the population that reproduces the consumption patterns of core countries is small. Furthermore, this segment does not seem to grow significantly with industrialization. The root of the problem is simple: the income level of core countries' populations is, on average, about ten times higher than that of populations in peripheral countries. In peripheral countries, therefore, the minority who reproduce the lifestyles of core countries must enjoy an income that is about ten times higher than the per capita income of their own countries. More precisely: with respect to the peripheral country in question, the highest proportion of its population that can have access to the lifestyles of core countries is 10%. In this extreme situation, the rest of the population—the other 90%—could not survive, since their income would be zero. In the typical manifestation of this kind of situation in the periphery, between one-third and half of the income is appropriated by the minority that reproduces the patterns of life of core countries, and the rest (between half and two-thirds) is divided more or less unequally among the mass of the population. In these cases, the privileged minority cannot be much more than 5% of the country's population.

The 5% of privileged people in the periphery corresponds, at the moment, to 85 million people. Consequently, the portion of the population that exercises real pressure on resources comes to 885 million. In the context of the projections we made, this subgroup of the population would reach 1.88 billion within a century. In this way, while the population of the capitalist world would increase 5.9 times, that of the portion of the population that actually exercises pressure on resources would increase 2.1 times. If the population exerting strong pressure on resources doubles—and, furthermore, if the average income of this population also doubles before reaching the relative saturation point in the utilization of nonrenewable resources— we must concede that this pressure will very likely grow by about four times over the course of the next century. It is worth adding that this pressure, now four times larger, will be exerted on a substantially smaller supply of resources. However, it would be unrealistic to think that a growth rate of this magnitude in resource pressure constitutes something outside man's capacity to control, even under the hypothesis that technology continues to be oriented by private companies in its conception and utilization. This statement does not imply ignoring that this is a considerable pressure, but it is worth highlighting that part of the increased pressure will be exerted on resources currently located in the system's periphery.

Another important fact to underscore is the growing clout of the privileged minority in peripheral countries within the population group enjoying a high standard of living in the capitalist system. Currently less than 10%, the participation of this minority would likely exceed one-third in the projection we made. Now, if we take into account that peripheral States will very likely be in a position to appropriate a larger proportion of the whole system's income through appreciation of the nonrenewable resources and labor they export, the hypothesis we formulated about stability—those 5% that would constitute the privileged group—should be considered a minimum. If the improvement in the terms of exchange allows for the 5% to grow to 10%, the privileged minority of the periphery would numerically exceed the population of the system's center. This tendency would also function to reduce resource pressure, since the increase in the number of those with access to high levels of consumption means that growth is happening with an aim toward greater distribution of already-familiar standards of consumption.

The relative increase in the number of privileged people from peripheral countries does not, however, prevent the perpetuation or deepening of the gulf that exists between them and the majority populations of their respective countries. In truth, if we look at the capitalist system as a whole, we see that the predominant evolutionary tendency is to exclude nine people out of ten from the principal benefits of development, and if we observe the group of peripheral countries in particular, we realize that the tendency there is to exclude nineteen out of twenty. This growing mass of those who are excluded (in absolute and in relative terms), which is concentrated in peripheral countries, constitutes in itself a weighty factor in the system's evolution. We cannot ignore the possibility that, in specific countries and also in general, changes in the system of political power may happen due to the pressure of these masses, with fundamental alterations in terms of the general orientation of the development process. Whatever new relationships may exist between the States of peripheral countries and large companies, the new orientation of development would have to be in a much more egalitarian direction, favoring collective forms of consumption and reducing the waste caused by the extreme diversification of privileged groups' current patterns of private consumption. Under this hypothesis, the pressure on resources would very likely be reduced.

The horizon of evolutionary possibilities that opens to peripheral countries is undoubtedly wide. At one extreme is sketched the possibility of the persistence of the tendencies that have held sway over the past quarter-century—toward intense concentration of income for the benefit of a reduced minority. In the center, there is the strengthening of the bureaucracies that control peripheral States—a tendency that has become more common in recent history and that leads to persistent improvements in the terms of exchange and to the expansion of the privileged minority, to the detriment of the system's center. At the other extreme, there arises the possibility of fundamental political changes, under the pressure of the growing masses who are excluded from the fruits of development, which would move toward effecting substantive changes in the orientation of the development process. This third possibility, combined with persistent improvements in the terms of exchange, corresponds to the least pressure on resources, just as the persistence of current tendencies toward income concentration generates the most pressure.

The general conclusion that arises is that the hypothesis of extending the forms of consumption that currently prevail in core countries to the whole of the capitalist system does not have a place inside the evolutionary possibilities apparent in this system. And this is the reason why a cataclysmic rupture, on a foreseeable horizon, lacks plausibility. The primary interest of the model that leads to this forecast of cataclysmic rupture is that it provides a thorough demonstration that the lifestyle created by industrial capitalism will always be the privilege of a minority. The cost of this lifestyle, in terms of degradation to the physical world, is so high that any attempt to generalize it would inevitably lead to the collapse of an entire civilization, putting at risk the survival of the human species. We have, then, thorough evidence that *economic development*—the idea that *poor peoples* can one day enjoy the lifestyles of currently *rich peoples*—is simply unattainable. We now know, incontrovertibly, that peripheral economies will never be *developed*, in the sense of being similar to the economies that currently make up the center of the capitalist system. But how can we ignore the fact that this idea has been very useful in mobilizing peripheral peoples and leading them to accept enormous sacrifices to legitimize the destruction of *archaic* forms of culture, to *explain* and make them *understand* the *necessity* of destroying the physical environment, to justify forms of dependence that reinforce the predatory character of the productive system? It is therefore necessary to affirm that the idea of economic development is simply a myth. Thanks to this idea, it has been possible to divert attention from the basic task of identifying fundamental collective necessities, and from the possibilities that the advance of science opens up to humankind. Instead, it has concentrated people's attention on abstract objectives, such as *investments*, *exports*, and *growth*. The primary importance of the model of *The Limits to Growth* is that it has contributed—albeit unintentionally—to destroying this myth, surely one of the pillars of the doctrine that enshrouds the domination of the peoples of peripheral countries within the new structure of the capitalist system.

Notes

1.The Prophecy of Collapse

1 My purpose here is not to address the epistemology of the social sciences. Since Dilthey, we have known that the social sciences "grew in the environment of the practice of life" (Wilhelm Dilthey, *Introduction à l'étude des sciences humaines*, Paris: PUF, 1942, p. 34). And Max Weber clearly demonstrated how the "comprehensive explanation" and the "explanatory comprehension" of social processes complement each other. Myth introduces a discriminating element into the spirit that unsettles the act of comprehension, which consists, according to Weber, in "grasping, through interpretation, the meaning or the signifying grouping that one has in one's view" (Max Weber, *Economie et société*, Paris: Plon, 1971, t. I, p. 8). See also J. Freund, *Les theories des sciences humaines*, Paris: Presses Universitaires de France, 1973.

2 D. H. Meadows, Dennis L. Meadows, Jorgen Randers, William W. Behrens III, *The Limits to Growth*, New York: Potomac Associates, 1972. And, for methodology, J. W. Forrester, *World Dynamics*, Cambridge, Mass.: Wright-Allen Press, 1971.

3 Based on the notable studies performed in recent years, in 1972 the United States Department of the Interior published a series of projections about the demand for basic products in the U.S. economy through the end of the century, indicating its probable degree of *dependence* with regard to external sources. According to these projections, for all but 1 of the 13 principal minerals the U.S. economy depends on to operate (the exception being phosphates) more than half of their annual consumption will be supplied by external sources by the end of the century. In 1985, 9 of the 13 products will already be in this situation, while in 1970 only 5 depended primarily on external sources. A product such as copper, a traditional item in U.S. exports and in 1970 still totally supplied by internal sources, will, by the end of the century, be more than 60 percent imported. Sulfur, another classic U.S. export product, will be in the exact same situation. However, the most dramatic case is that of petroleum: having been the greatest global exporter, the United States is moving toward becoming one of its greatest importers. According to the Department of Commerce, U.S. imports of petroleum in 1985 will very likely be four times those of 1970 and, by the end of the century, they will be eight times greater. True, these calculations did not take into account the effects of the considerable increase in relative prices for petroleum that would occur in the last quarter of 1973. If we take into account this rise in prices, the projected value of U.S. petroleum imports in 1985 would equal twice the total of all U.S. imports in 1970.

4 [*Tr.*] In other words, these projections do not take into account that the resources available in the world are finite and can only sustain growth for so long.

5 [*Tr.*] That is, they acknowledged that the world's resources are finite and provided estimates to try to quantify those resources.

6 One of the few economists who has seriously concerned himself with this problem, Professor Georgescu-Roegen, tells us: "Some economists have alluded to the fact that

man can neither create nor destroy matter or energy—a truth which follows from the Principle of Conservation of Matter-Energy, alias the First Law of Thermodynamics. Yet no one seems to have been struck by the question— so puzzling in the light of this law—'what then does the economic process do?' ... [L]et us consider the economic process as a whole and view it only from the purely physical viewpoint. What we must note first of all is that this process is a partial process which, like all partial processes, is circumscribed by a boundary across which matter and energy are exchanged with the rest of the material universe. The answer to the question of what this *material* process does is simple: it neither produces nor consumes matter-energy; it only absorbs matter-energy and throws it out continuously.... We may trust that even the fiercest partisan of the position that natural resources have nothing to do with value will admit in the end that there is a difference between what goes into the economic process and what comes out of it. ... From the viewpoint of thermodynamics, matter-energy enters the economic process in a state of *low entropy* and comes out of it in a state of *high entropy*." N. Georgescu-Roegen, *The Entropy Law and the Economic Problem*, conference address given at the University of Alabama, 1970. See also, from the same author, *The Entropy Law and the Economic Process*, Cambridge, Mass.: Harvard University Press, 1971.

2. The Structural Evolution of the Capitalist System

1 The authors of *The Limits to Growth* are explicit about their adopted methodology: "The basis of the method," they say, "is the recognition that the *structure* of any system—the many circular, interlocking, sometimes time-delayed relationships among its components—is often

just as important in determining its behavior as the individual components themselves" (p. 31). And, later on, they add, a "high level of aggregation is necessary at this point to keep the model understandable…. National boundaries are not recognized. Distribution inequalities of food, resources, and capital are included implicitly in the data but they are not calculated explicitly nor graphed in the output" (p. 94).

2 *The Limits to Growth*, p. 109.

3 [*Tr.*] Rostow believed it was exceptionally difficult for countries to skip phases of economic development—they were obliged to pass through the various stages (in order) before they could become "developed."

4 Regarding the specificity of delayed industrialization in Europe, particularly with regard to its institutional aspects, see the classic work of A. Gerschenkron, *Economic Backwardness in Historical Perspective*, Cambridge, Mass.: Harvard University Press, 1966, primarily on pages 5–50. See also B. Gille, "Banking and Industrialization in Europe, 1870–1914," and B. Supple, "The State and the Industrial Revolution, 1700–1914," in *The Industrial Revolution*, directed by Carlo M. Chipolla, 3rd volume of *The Fontana Economic History of Europe*, London: Collins/Fontana Books, 1973.

5 To date, the period of most rapid growth for international commerce was 1840–1870, during which the English global economic project reached its height, when the growth rate reached the anual average of 13 percent. Cf. A. H. Imlah, *Economic Elements in the Pax Britannica* (Cambridge, Mass.: Harvard University Press, 1958), p. 190, and also A. G. Kenwood and A. L. Lougheed, *The Growth of the International Economy 1820–1960* (London: Unwin Ltd., 1971), p. 90. However, until the turn of the century, international commerce would continue to grow more rapidly than production in the global economy as a whole. The structural changes geared toward greater internal integration of national economic systems, which became more visible in the

last two decades of that century, would only have repercussions on the behavior of the international economy
during the current century. In essence, beginning with
this century's first decade and continuing through 1950,
global commerce of manufactured goods would grow
less rapidly than the production of these goods. See A.
Maizels, *Industrial Growth and World Trade* (London:
National Institute of Economics and Social Research,
1963, pp. 139–140 and 388).

6 [*Tr.*] In other words, rival companies come to mutually
beneficial agreements about prices, products, etc., in
order to maximize their profits.

7 [*Tr.*] The process of substituting products previously
imported from abroad with domestic products.

8 In places where modernizing the infrastructure required
importing equipment (the case of railroads, for example),
investments tended to be considerable and necessitated
external cooperation. However, the reduction in the
capacity to import, which resulted from subsequent
indebtedness, would only be felt in the longer term.

9 [*Tr.*] A series of international agreements aimed at facili-
tating economic relations between member countries.

10 A summary of the data related to this process can be found
in *Multinational Corporations in World Development*,
New York: United Nations, 1973. For a systematic bibliography on this topic see R. Vernon, *Sovereignty at Bay*
(1971), Penguin edition, 1973.

11 A classic example of tutelage exerted by the banking
system is found in the process of German industrialization. See note 4 from this section and, for a discussion
of the remnants of this tutelage, see A. Shonfield, *Modern
Capitalism*, Oxford: Oxford University Press, 1965, pp.
239–297.

12 Cf. C. Furtado, *A Hegemonia dos Estados Unidos e o
Subdesenvolvimento da América Latina* (Rio: Civilização
Brasileira, 1973) pp. 43–51, and J. Fred Weston,
"Conglomerate Firms," in *Economics of Industrial
Structure*, edited by Basil S. Yamey (Harmondsworth:

Penguin, 1973), which contains a selective bibliography on this topic.

13 [Tr.] The idea that the more of a certain product you make, the lower the cost will be per individual product.

14 [Tr.] That is, economies of scale require large investments in things like equipment, production plants, etc., which makes it harder for newcomers to succeed in these markets.

15 Naturally, financial coordination can be taken far beyond that of oligopolistic coordination. This kind of coordination only makes sense to the extent that it offers operational advantages and allows the production and investment plans of each company with administrative autonomy to be aligned. Financial coordination, by allowing one branch of activity to subsidize another or finance its expansion, can (theoretically) be extended indefinitely. Situated at a very general decision-making level, the diseconomies of scale are practically nonexistent in this case. Recent studies done in the United States suggest that financial coordination is much more widely practiced than is generally supposed. Without assuming the institutional form it has in Germany, where the existence of the *Aufsichtsrat* (the company's supervisory board) allows banks to ostensibly take part in the orientation of the company, the interweaving of supervisory committees and the control of a small fraction of the voting capital (no more than 5 percent) have transformed U.S. banks into control centers for economic activity as a whole, whose importance can scarcely be exaggerated. Thus, according to information divulged by the Subcommittee on Banking and Currency of the U.S. Congress, in 1971 banks held in their portfolios $577 billion dollars of bonds issued by anonymous societies and managed funds that controlled an additional $336 billion dollars in the form of similar financial bonds.

16 Between 1965 and 1972 the number of branches of U.S. banks abroad grew from 303 to 1,009; with respect to large banks headquartered in New York, the proportion

of foreign deposits grew from 8.5 percent (of national deposits) to 65.5 percent between 1960 and 1972. See *Multinational Corporations in World Development*, cit. p. 12. The international expansion of the banking network of other core countries has been equally considerable, particularly in the case of Japan. The external operations of a large company are, as a rule, ostensibly directed by an "international" subsidiary located in whichever country is most convenient, even though the decision-making center remains in the company's country of origin.

17 We prefer to use the simple term "large company" to refer to what it is increasingly common to designate a "multinational corporation." In the current capitalist economy, each large company—with the exception of public services—is "international," in the sense that it acts simultaneously in various countries, whether through commercial subsidiaries, through subsidiary producers, or through participation in producing companies. Its scale requires internationalization, even if the company has its capital controlled by a National State. On the other hand, a medium-size or large company that has restricted international involvement, by virtue of the fact that it acts internally at the level of oligopolies, must follow the "international" behavior of the oligopoly as a whole. In summary: the difference between "national" and "international" tends to be secondary; what matters most is the relative clout of the company.

18 The U.S. proposals of 1972 aimed at differentiating the levels of decision-making, which would mean institution-alizing what we see in practice—that is, that the other countries of the capitalist world do not have effective means at their disposal to move a "planetary" policy forward by themselves—are an indication of the system's evolutionary tendency in the current decade. The two largest industrial nations after the United States, due precisely to the fact that they are located on the edges of the system—Germany on the one hand and Japan on the other—could influence the political evolution of the

United States. However, these two nations are profoundly dependent on the current evolutionary model of the capitalist world to move forward with the extraordinary economic expansion they are enjoying. On the economic level, these two nations are those who benefit most from a defense system to which they contribute the least.

19 [*Tr.*] After the dollar became the global reserve currency, the U.S. was no longer limited by the need to back every dollar in gold and was therefore able to print more currency (and take on more debt).

3. Large Companies in New Center–Periphery Relations

1 [*Tr.*] Whereas today's developed countries went through a period of gradual industrialization in which technology evolved in tandem with economic stability, peripheral countries today have little chance to go through a similar process because large companies' actions prevent their national economies from becoming autonomous and stable.

2 [*Tr.*] The amount of innovation, flexibility, and reinvention that happens in an economy and that helps it evolve and grow over time.

3 [*Tr.*] In other words, in peripheral countries wealth is very unequally divided—a very small percentage of the population has great wealth, while the vast majority of the population has very few financial resources.

4 [*Tr.*] That is to say, even though some economic activities may involve various countries, they are all contained within the operations of a single company.

5 [*Tr.*] Here Furtado refers to companies' ability to manipulate prices and operations so that they are unaffected (or only minimally affected) by changes in official exchange rates.

6 [*Tr.*] In other words, a company can only increase sales in a particular market up to a certain point; after that,

in order to make more money it must decrease the cost of its labor, which may be done by outsourcing labor to different countries.

7 Strictly speaking, the expansion of large companies is not restricted to the realm of the capitalist system; economic relations between the capitalist system and socialist economies continue to be of an essentially commercial nature, without their impeding these transactions from being performed more and more through large companies. Furthermore, agreements on industrial cooperation are being signed in growing numbers (about 600, by 1973) between governments of socialist countries and large companies from the capitalist world. These agreements very rarely involve participation in these companies' capital (although limited participation has been permitted in Romania and Hungary and, even earlier, in Yugoslavia); this participation is generally linked to the creation of a flow of exports to capitalist countries, care of these large companies. See the United Nations Economic Commission for Europe, *Analytical Report on Industrial Cooperation among ECE Countries* (Geneva: United Nations, 1973).

8 [*Tr.*] Even the U.S., despite its hegemonic position and influence, cannot do whatever it wants; other countries, economies, and large companies can take actions that pressure the U.S. to act (or not act) in certain ways.

9 [*Tr.*] In other words, nation-states and large companies can both exert a certain amount of influence and contribute to national autonomy, but they must also be responsive to the structures of power that can push them in one way or another if they challenge the status quo too much.

10 [*Tr.*] The International Telephone & Telegraph company supported the right-wing Chilean group that staged a *coup d'état* in 1973, resulting in the suicide of then-president Salvador Allende and the rise of Augusto Pinochet to power.

4. Options for Peripheral Countries

1 [*Tr.*] That is, as large companies began to influence the governments of peripheral countries, explicit colonialism became unnecessary and was phased out.

2 See figures 29 and 39 of *The Limits to Growth*, op. cit.

3 [*Tr.*] Although peripheral States are at a disadvantage when it comes to coordinating economic activities with each other, the example of OPEC (the Organization of the Petroleum Exporting Countries), founded in 1960, is an example of successful cooperation among peripheral countries.

4 [*Tr.*] For example, unless there is elaborate coordination between all peripheral countries, if one peripheral country raises the price of its labor, large companies can simply move their operations to another country with cheap labor.

5 [*Tr.*] The difference in wages earned between workers in one industry in comparison to workers in another industry, or between workers in the same industry in different locations.

Index